How to Write a Brilliant Novel

Workbook

Written by RITA-Award Winning, Bests-Selling Novelist

Susan May Warren

Published by My Book Therapy, a division of Susan May Warren Fiction, LLC, 20 Wild Plum Dr., Grand Marais, MN 55604. (218)387-2853. First Edition.

ISBN: 978-0-9910114-8-3

Visit our Web site at www.learnhowtowriteanovel.com for information on more resources for writers.

To receive instruction on writing, or further help with writing projects via My Book Therapy's boutique fiction editing services, contact info@mybooktherapy.com

What people are saying about My Book Therapy/Learn How To Write a Novel

"A quirky, fun, practical guide from a writer who knows what she's doing." ~ **James Scott Bell,** bestselling author of Write Great Fiction: Plot & Structure.

Writing my novel was like traveling in a foreign land without a map. I'd see beautiful things and meet great people, but never get to my destination. Now I have the map I need. Learning the craft of structure was extremely important for me, freeing precious time to spend on character development and storyworld. ~ **Julie Matuska**

About Susan May Warren's teaching:

"If word of mouth sells, Susie May Warren will be swamped. Since working with her I've told author friends non-stop about *Book Therapy.* Passionate. Funny. And knock-down-drag-out brilliant at launching my writing to another stratosphere." ~ **Jim Rubart**, best-selling, Christy-award wining author of *Rooms*

I have taken other fiction writing workshops before, but Susan's acronyms and explanations made it click this time. Susan covered the basics (and then some) in a fun and engaging way. And I can apply this knowledge to my project immediately. I'm confident I can write my novel now without overlooking any aspect of plot, characters or scenes. ~ **M. C. Scott** (www.michelecscott.com and www.mommyforward.com)

Susan May Warren's class is an incredible experience which I would definitely suggest to any unpublished writers looking to get published or for beginning authors wanted to learn how to write a novel. ~ **C. Fontenelle**

Learning the craft of writing occurs at many different levels. Susan holds the hand of the beginning writer, explains the craft, helps him/her visualize the craft in movies and books, and most importantly, points it out in the writing of the participant. ~ **R. Schmeckpeper**

Susan May Warren's instruction through hands on writing sessions allowed me to learn and apply at my own pace. Practical and Inspiring teaching to feed the writer's pen and soul. ~ **Michelle Lim**, Agented author and ACFW Genesis winner

What can feel like an overwhelming endeavor became a step by step process that helps a seat-of-the pantser like me stay on track. ~ **Kimberly Buckner**, 2014 Maggie award winner

About Advanced Fiction Writing:

" If you're intending to write a best-selling novel, I can think of no better place to start than with Susan May Warren's *Advanced Fiction Writing*. This is a book for those who need to dig into the techniques of writing -- not just hear the happy-talk, big-picture stuff that is so often heard at conferences. If you really want to get into the nuts and bolts of writing strong fiction, then this is for you. Clear, practical advice from an award-winning novelist."
– **Chip MacGregor**, Literary Agent, MacGregor Literary

About the My Book Therapy Premium Membership for Advanced Writers:

"I am quite possibly one of MBT's biggest proponents *ever* because of how its impacted my writing journey. The retreats are fabulous, so I'd highly encourage premium members to take advantage of their retreat discount and attend. The learning combined with sooo many laughs is worth every penny and minute. I hugely depend on the MBT website. I can't tell you how many times I've searched the site for articles to help with this or that aspect of my story. I'm not always able to attend every pep talk due to my schedule, so I love that after the fact, I still have access to them. I read the flash blog every day. Also, I've worked through every MBT workbook--Inside Out, Deep & Wide, Kiss & Tell--and am pretty sure I will never write another book without the MBT Book Buddy! It's so much help in getting to know your characters and developing your plot." ~ **Melissa Tagg**, Multi-published author

"I am an MBT Premium member, and I wouldn't give it up for anything. In September, an editor requested a proposal for a romance. Never thought about writing a romance. I immediately went to the MBT Locker Room and researched the Library for articles on writing romances. In August I started out with an idea. The library and the MBT *Kiss and Tell* workbook provided the help I needed, and in December I wrote *The End* and sent it off. I also utilize the webinars and Peptalks by Susie and Rachel. Mini-conferences every month!" ~ **Pat Trainum**, Multi-published author

Write the novel you've always wanted to write!

Award-winning authors Susan May Warren and Rachel Hauck have taken their *My Book Therapy* techniques and compiled them into one comprehensive book for the first-time novelist. From step by step instruction to top-secret tips, they help the aspiring novelist discover, create, and publish the novel hidden inside them.

About the Author:

Susan May Warren

Susan May Warren is the Christy, RITA and Carol award-winning author of over forty-five novels with Tyndale, Barbour, Steeple Hill and Summerside Press. A prolific novelist with over 1 million books sold, Susan has written contemporary and historical romances, romantic-suspense, thrillers, rom-com and Christmas novellas. She loves to help people launch their writing careers and is the founder of www.MyBookTherapy.com and www.LearnHowtoWriteaNovel.com, a writing website that helps authors get published and stay published. She's also the author of the popular writing method, *The Story Equation*. Find excerpts and reviews of her novels at www.susanmaywarren.com

Dedication:

For your glory, Lord

To everyone who has ever attended one of my classes, encouraged me, and suggested I write a book—this is for you.

Acknowledgements

To the My Book Therapy Voices for their encouragement and questions. You make me a better writer and teacher.

To Steve Laube for walking me through the world of self-publishing! You rock.

To Rachel, *my* Therapist.
You are brilliant.

Finally, to Andrew, and my family.
You make me feel like a rock star.

Susan May Warren

Table of Contents

If you've always wanted to write a novel, this book is for you

We all have goals, right? Dreams, desires, hopes that have been niggling at us for years. For aspiring authors, it's the dream of writing a novel. You're a writer if every time you hear an interesting job description or read a compelling story in the newspaper, you think, "Hey, that would make an interesting premise for a novel." You're a writer if, when you get introduced to someone new, you can't help but ask about their lives, and can barely resist the urge to take out a pen and some paper and jot down some notes. You're a writer if, when you're reading a novel, you occasionally take a breath and say, "Wow, I want to write like that."

If you're a writer, this book is for you.

I remember the day when I decided to write a novel. I was in Siberia, in the middle of a solemn and icy winter. I had four children, all under the age of six, and my husband was gone, again, planting a church. I had read everything in the house at least twice, and I decided that my imagination could do at least as well as one of the books I'd devoured in a day. (Boy, did I have much to learn!) I sat down at the computer and said, "I'm writing a book."

That's about as far as I got. Once I actually sat down and stared at the computer, I *had not idea how a book was put together*. Where did I start? How did I develop characters? What was my point? And most importantly—how did I get the story from my brain to the computer and into print?

It took me a year of writing, first on Saturdays, and then every day. But I finished my first book. To all who think that I then ran out and found a publisher—not! Four books later . . . .

What I learned through that first novel was:
1. Writing a good novel was harder than I thought, and I needed a lot of work.
2. I love to write, and was willing to make the journey, whatever it took.
3. Even if I never got published, God could use my writing journey for good in my life.

A writer's life is solitary, hard work, fraught with rejection, frustration, and even envy. *But*, if you look at at the journey as another way that you will grow and experience your world, then it's a journey that is ripe with rewards.

This is the book I wish I had when I first started. It's because of those years of angst and study that I started *My Book Therapy*, a blog about how to write and a fiction editing service to help writers along the way. When I first started writing, I was in *Siberia*. As in *Russia*. Alone. Just me, some novels, and my imagination. I wished I had a reference guide, something to organize all the information I needed in one place, maybe a step by step journey, and a companion/encourager to help me complete my dream. Sure, I had writing books, but they made the process so *complicated*. I knew it had to be easier. *Inside . . . Out* is my writing manual—what I developed and now use to create stories. It's my successes, my systems . . . and my secrets. And, as a bonus, you also get the perspective of Rachel Hauck, my pal and *My Book Therapy* partner, thrown in to add another rich perspective. It's our manual of writing the books we know how to write.

How to use this book:

There are three steps to your writing journey:

- **Discovering** the story you want to write. There's a lot of talking to yourself during this process, so if you have an office with a lock on the door, that helps!
- **Creating** the story. This is the long part, so arm yourself with coffee, a notepad, a computer, and chocolate chips, not necessarily in that order.
- **Publishing** the story. This is understanding the nuts and bolts of the industry.

How to Write a Brilliant Novel is divided into these three sections, with step by step instruction on how to complete each of these legs of the journey. If you spend one hour a week reading and doing the exercises at the end of each lesson, you'll slowly create that novel stirring in your heart (or head), and you'll finish it in a year.

Along the way, you'll learn everything from writing life management, story structure, characterization, and some easy plotting methods, including how to create the perfect Black Moment and life-changing Epiphany. You'll learn how to build a novel scene by scene, and how to create those scenes. You'll get editing hints, and learn how to package your manuscript into a proposal that will catch the eye of an agent or editor. And, if you stick with this book to the very end, maybe you'll even see your novel on a bookshelf at Barnes and Noble. I hope so! I'm blessed to be able to share the stories inside me with the world out there. I hope they inspire and encourage, delight and challenge others.

I pray this book helps you discover the writer in you.

You CAN write something Brilliant!

The Writer's Life

No one starts a journey without gathering their supplies, stretching out, and getting into shape. At least, you shouldn't! Before you write one word, one hint of "Once Upon a Time"—and I know you're itching to do so, but I promise it'll be worth the wait!—let's spend a few moments packing our gear.

I met my husband in the boundary waters canoe area of Minnesota. I was a camp director. He was a trail guide. We both loved the outdoors. I knew we were headed for a lifetime of camping and outdoor fun. Then our four children came along, time passed, and our oldest was fifteen by the time we realized they had never been on a canoe trip. So after we'd moved home from Russia, we decided to pack them up and take them out into the wilderness.

We planned a simple trip—six to eight miles of canoeing a day, three portages a day (a few uphill, but we were tough), and plenty of food and fun. We even decided to take my parents. We had three canoes, ten packs, and a lot of enthusiasm.

We left early on a Saturday morning, our paddles dipping into a pristine lake that mirrored the fat, happy clouds above. We sang a little song. A loon sang back. My children smiled, and I laughed in the face of our adventure.

Two days, three lakes, a rainstorm, and four million-mile portages later, I wasn't laughing any longer. Whose stupid idea was it anyway to go out and fight with the bugs and the mud? Who said I could carry a canoe, huh?

We were out of shape, overburdened, hot, tired, hungry, smelly, and there may have been a few ugly attitudes. I had to face the truth: I'd turned into a wimp. I simply didn't have the staying power to finish our trip. I wanted to sprawl on the rooted ground until the forest service guys found me and choppered me home. The good news is, after a granola bar and a pep talk, I shouldered my canoe and pressed on, singing "Amazing Grace," believing someday the portages would end. They did, and we have the pictures of happy, grimy campers gracing our kitchen wall to prove it.

Writing a book is like that canoe trip. Your first chapter is beautiful and fun. You write it and read it aloud, laughing with joy at your magnificent prose. But by chapter seven, your character is uncooperative, hopelessly lost—or worse, has already solved his problem. Your head hurts from all the red and green squiggly lines (for those who use Microsoft Word), and there are storm clouds brewing in your head. You just want to turn back. (Please, please don't hit delete!) You think: *What made me believe I could write a novel, anyway?*

Today, while the skies are still blue and clear, and the lake pristine, I want you to take a deep look inside yourself and decide. Do you have the resolve to say, "Hey, I'm a writer. I'm on a journey. And I'm not going to quit until I get there, regardless of the pitfalls, the frustrations, and the fact that somewhere down the road, even my family may look at me and say, '*Are you sure*?'"

It's in the easy times that you need to resolve not to quit in the hard times. Writing a book is, well, like a canoe portage. One foot in front of the other, swatting away the bugs, enduring the pain and the sweat, believing that, eventually, you'll get to the blue skies at the end.

And I promise, it's worth it.

Raise your "write" hand and repeat after me: *I am a writer. And I promise not to quit until I've written "The End."*

Now you may proceed.

Four Keys to a Writer's Life

As you prep for your journey, I want you to start exercising! You're going to get in shape! Work off the dust of your minds and tighten the flab of your daily schedules so you can utilize the writing time you have in your days.

Writing is much like every other discipline. It takes **commitment.** After all, as much as we'd like it to happen, those books don't just download from our brains automatically! It takes **nurturing.** Did you know that your brain has a well of words for each day, and you need to replenish those words after you use them? It takes **time** (something we're going to figure out how to get!), and it takes a **game plan**.

Commitment: The fact is, writing will take you away from your family, your health club, your church, your social groups, your online gaming, your Sudoku, your television . . . you get my drift. There are costs. The keys to keeping those costs in line are:

1. Priorities
2. Balance
3. Perspective

Writing should *always* come after spending time with God (that's also the nurturing part!) and rarely before family and church, but sometimes writing does come before workouts and social life.

My friend Judy Baer, writing coach extraordinaire, shared this illustration with me: "Stand on one foot and balance. You can't stand perfectly still, but rather, you have to lean to different sides to keep your balance."

Writing and life should be like this—different sides require attention in different waves. If you are to invest in writing, then know that you might have to give up other things. Don't worry—it's not forever! Just for a while. If you were training for the Olympics, you'd have a training schedule, and it would ramp up when you had specific events to meet. Take a look at your life and see if you can carve out one hour per day, or three days per week to invest in writing. Then, put that on your calendar in *red*. Writing is an appointment. Be there.

Nurturing: Your brain needs a steady supply of new words, spiritual nourishment, research facts, and good writing to keep it fresh and ready to put prose on the page.

Spiritual Nourishment: Writing is largely a spiritual event. You are connecting on a thematic level with your reader, and that happens in the spiritual realm. Sure, we access many of these metaphors through emotion, but looking past feelings to their deeper meaning and sources helps broaden your understanding of your book, your character's journey, and, most importantly, *why* you are spending time writing this book. Make a habit of spending time soaking in God's Word, or a devotional book like *Streams in the Desert*, or whatever form of spiritual food you need for your diet. I like to read theology books, but sometimes a great devotional book puts my spirit into the right frame to see beyond myself, to tap into the bigger picture, and inspires me to write.

Research: Make it your goal to keep up with the world. Technology. Medicine. Trends. Don't be afraid to use the Discovery Channel for interesting plot ideas! Know what's happening in culture and politics. Read biographies, current and past—you'll be inspired with new story ideas. Subscribe to *Reader's Digest* and *National Geographic*. (At least TiVo the channel!) To communicate to our world, you need to understand it.

Read Up: Fill your mind with great writing. Start your writing time reading the Psalms, or perhaps a book of poetry. Read the classics, yes, but also make it your goal to read in your genre! Most importantly, find authors that are better than you and soak in their words, analyzing why they are fabulous writers. Feeding your mind and your soul will give you materials you can draw from as you create.

Time: This is one of the hardest areas for new writers to manage. Most of us don't have hours in the day to wait for the muse to find us. We have thirty minutes after supper, or perhaps three hours on a Saturday morning.

Here are a few strategies for maximizing that time:

1. *Plan ahead for your writing time and get your family to help you protect it.* I have a sign on my door that reads, "Cry Me a River." In other words, my family better have a good reason to come through that door when it's closed. Only if there's blood or fire is the general rule. When my children were young, I always had an open door policy. However, I asked them to respect my time, just like I respected theirs. That meant that I spent time with them first—reading, helping with homework, fixing dinner—whatever they needed. I also involved them in the writing process. If they allowed me to finish a chapter, we'd celebrate with something fun. Yes, there was a lot of ice cream in those early days. And I promised that when my first book got published, I'd take them to Disney World. I kept that promise. Enlisting your family's help will free you from guilt *and* give them an opportunity to share in your victories as you write. Make your family your partners.

2. *Keep a notebook of ideas.* Dialogue, new characters, plot twists will invariably come to you as you wash dishes, walk the dog, clean the bathroom, drive to work, sit in a boring meeting, or even in the middle of the night. Sometimes you can't dash to your computer to put in that perfect sentence, so put it in your notebook. You'll have a collection of words and sentences to jumpstart your creativity when you sit down to write.

3. *Don't clean up your writing space mid-project.* Okay, I know, that sounds like a messy person's excuse. But if you simply walk away from your computer after you finish a scene, you'll be able to slip right back into the scene when you come back.

Have a special room to write in so you can close the door, even if it's a section of your bedroom—something I did for years. I had a little garage-sale chair with a pile of books on the opposite side of the bed—my little alcove. But, if you can't find a separate space, invest in a little basket to throw all your writing gear in (research books, books on writing), and then set it in a place where it won't be "reorganized," as my husband calls it. Keeping your research handy helps you maximize your time when you sit down and dive back into your story.

Game Plan: I'm not talking plotting versus seat-of-the-pants writing here. I'm talking about a little journal that you keep *after* your writing session. Write down any thoughts you have for the next chapter, as well as your goal for the next writing session. Maybe you want to go back and revise the previous chapter, or fix certain words. Maybe you need more research. Maybe you just want to plow ahead, but have notes for revisions.

Keeping a journal of your writing time helps you focus on each writing session without having to ask, "Now, where was I?" This is especially true if a week or more has gone by in between writing sessions.

I know some of you who have little children are thinking, "Hey, I don't even have time to wash my hair—I can't possibly find time to write." Let's see, greasy hair versus seeing your dreams come true. You can wash your hair when your kids go to school. *No*, I'm not *that* bad! I like clean hair, but I well remember the days when I typed with my children on my lap, or stayed up late with my laptop while my husband snoozed beside me.

He sure woke up when I got that first contract.

I am a writer. And I promise not to quit until I've written "The End."

Say it until you mean it. And then turn the page.

Keep away from people who try to belittle your ambitions. Small people always do that but the really great ones make you feel that you, too, can become great.

Mark Twain

Step One: Discover

Where do you start?

I love *Dancing with the Stars*. Mostly because they take regular people (okay, *stars*) and teach them how to dance. So I took a dancing class. And realized I was in over my head. I just don't move like dancers do. And there are so many different styles and music types. But the thing is, I do have rhythm, so I *could* learn to dance, and eventually, dance from the soul. First, however, I had to focus on the kind of dancing I wanted to learn, get down the basic steps, and practice.

So, you have an idea, a feeling, perhaps a character that has been roaming around your head for awhile, nudging you to develop a story. That's a great place to start, but don't put that pen to paper yet. First: What *kind* of book will you write? Think of it as dancing the Tango: You want to Tango, but you have to learn the beat of the music and the basic steps first.

So, what genre of book do you want to write?
Here's a hint: *Take a look at what you're already reading.* If you hate sci-fi, and your TBR (to be read) pile is stocked with John Grisham legal thrillers, chances are you won't know how to craft a good sci-fi story.

Books fall into segmented genres. Take a walk through the bookstore and check out the plethora of genres represented. Your book will fall inside one of these sections. Look at the main headings:
> Romance
> Mysteries or Thrillers
> Women's fiction
> Chick Lit
> Sci-Fi
> Fantasy
> Memoirs
> Young Adult

Within those main headings, you'll find variations:
> Romantic Suspense
> Romantic Comedy

And within those, even further variations: Historical, Contemporary, etc. Each genre, and the subgenres within them, encompasses particular elements.
For example:
> Romance: Hero/heroine have to meet by chapter 3 (preferably chapter 1), they must have a Black Moment, they must have a happy ending.
> Fantasy: Must have real-world rules we can understand.
> Suspense: Must have an Ignition and a Ticking Time Bomb (or deadline).
> Thriller: The format of the story is concentrated on what could happen to the characters.
> Mystery: The dead body is at the beginning, and the focus is on what happened.

Learning these elements will be key to learning how to structure your novel.

How do you find these elements?
- ✓ **READ.** Read your favorite authors, and then dissect their books to find out what works and what doesn't. I keep a journal of all the books I read and refer to it when I'm lost or confused or feeling overwhelmed. T.S. Eliot wrote: "A poor poet imitates, a good poet steals." Now, I'm not advocating plagiarism, but finding out what elements in others' work you enjoy will help you in developing your own voice.
- ✓ **Study particular elements of that craft.** Buy a genre-particular writing book, such as the kind offered by Writer's Digest.
- ✓ **Write and write and write and get feedback**. Join a critique group. It's essential to get honest feedback from people you trust.

What do you know? Your book is going to take research. I often write books about people or professions or places I'd like to visit or know about, because it forces me to do research, which I love. But my first books were written about a place I knew, with characters I'd met, and a theme close to my heart.

Everyone has something unique about them—their past, their education, their profession, their experiences, their culture, their interests. You are unique. And you will bring this unique perspective to your writing. It's from this place that you'll develop your platform for writing.

See, as we get further along, I'm going to ask: *Why* should someone pick up your book and spend the next few hours reading it? What makes your book unique and why are *you* the one to tell the story?

Are you a cop, telling stories about protecting the homeland?
Are you a nurse, writing the next *ER* series?
Are you an archeologist, discovering the secrets of time?
Are you a former CIA agent, unfolding the past?

More and more, agents and editors want someone who has a platform, someone who can give resonance to their story. With non-fiction, this is a no-brainer, but with fiction, that person can be harder to find. After all, I've never been a bull rider, so what could I possibly bring to a story like *Taming Rafe?* And, I've never been a Delta Force operative undercover in Taiwan, trying to rescue a kidnapped girl, so what authority could I possibly give to *Wiser than Serpents?*

Well, let's see. I lived in Taiwan and in Russia, and I know people who have known people who have "disappeared" into the world of human trafficking. I know friends who fought human trafficking, and I've had experience with being held against my will. I brought all these things to the storyline of *Wiser than Serpents*.

For *Taming Rafe*, I tapped into my love of all things cowboy, as well as my experience as a fundraiser and working with orphans overseas. I also spent time on a ranch, learning the ropes. (Pun intended!)

Even if you don't have a platform, you have a reason why you are uniquely created to write your story. Dee Henderson, one of my favorite authors, said to me years ago, "Find what you are good at, hone that, and create a niche for your writing." I chose Russia, and now out of my 45 novels and novellas, over half have some connection to Russia.

So, let's start with a list of things that you could write about.

Your Turn:

What are your favorite genres? Give a reason for each choice.

Ten unique things about yourself that you believe, have experienced, or know that you could write about:

1.

2.

3.

4.

5.

6.

7.

8.

9.

10.

Why Write a Novel?

As a reader, you can probably define what draws you to a book. As a writer, you need to keep that in mind as you create a plot. I know what I like in a —book—what kinds of professions and settings and plots—and those are reflected in the books I create. Other authors seek out different plots based on their interests. But in the end, we're all searching for some new perspective on life, a world to dive into, and something that delights our hearts. As you create your story, keep this in mind. Keep asking: *Why should someone read my book?* The answer should come from the following three functions of storytelling.

3 Functions of Storytelling:
  1. Entertainment
  2. To escape into a different world
  3. To understand, life, God, each other, ourselves.

I know you believe that your Staggering Work of Fiction is unique. That it's never been told before . . . um, okaaaay. Actually, it's never been told in *your* voice, in *your* style, but I have news for you:

There are six major plots in the world that all books follow. (Well, six that I've found. If you can find a new, different one, by all means, let me know!)

Basic plots connect with us in a way that holds our attention. Below, you'll find the six basic plots. The *best* stories, the epics, sometimes contain elements of all six plots, ending, as most of them do, with the hero and heroine brought together in perfect love and triumph of reaching the goal, the true happy ending.

Six Basic Plots

In dancing, there are the basics: the two-step, the waltz, the tango, etc. Everything else is a variation of these. Through all the storytelling in the world, a handful of basic plots reoccur, so much so that every story can be boiled down to one of these six plots (with variations, of course, on setting, characters and endings). If you've already developed a plot, see where yours fits in:

1. **Overcoming the Monster** – A hero on behalf of a greater good sets out to take on and slay some evil, deadly foe. We see this in movies like *Erin Brockovich, Jaws, Star Wars, The Firm, The Pelican Brief*, and one of my favorites, *Ferris Bueller's Day Off.* (He's overcoming the school principal!)
2. **Rags to Riches** – Someone faces external obstacles of society or personal opposition, and the story ends with her finding the real "riches" within herself, and in the end, getting her dreams. *Cinderella, My Fair Lady*, and *Pretty Woman* are examples of this.
3. **The Great Quest** – The story's about the journey, the friends made along the journey, and how they band together to accomplish the task, win the treasure, or the war. Examples are *Raiders of the Lost Ark, National Treasure, Saving Private Ryan*, and even *Amazing Race*.
4. **Home Again, Home Again** – Stories about people leaving the world they know, being changed by the experience, then taking those changes home and adapting them to their world. *Wizard of Oz, Sweet Home Alabama*
5. **Beast to Beauty** – A person is forced to go into a "prison" of some kind. They are finally redeemed, either by an outside liberator, or by personal enlightenment. *Snow White, The Sound of Music, The Mighty Ducks, Gladiator*

   A **Tragedy** is a takeoff of this type of plot without the happy ending. *Macbeth* or *A Beautiful Mind* shows what happens when the hero is sucked into a spell of darkness, the power of the ego. They initially might enjoy a dreamlike success, but in the end the dream turns to nightmare, and they are destroyed.
6. **See the Light** – The stories are about people who are forced to re-examine who they are, or are in the middle of a misunderstanding, and they must find a new perspective to come through it and see the light. *The Devil Wears Prada, Return to Me, Chasing Liberty*

Your Turn:

What is your favorite movie or book? Does it fit into one of the Six Basic Plots?

Study these plots. What makes them different from each other? What makes them the same?

Now, think about *your* idea. What plot does *it* fit? Answering this question will help you as you learn the *structure* of your novel.

Don't all books have essentially the same basic elements?

Yes, actually they do.

So, let's start with: What makes a great book?

The Four Things all **Stories** must **have:**

- ✓ Theme – What is the story about? What can we learn about ourselves or humanity or life or even God?

- ✓ Plot – What happens in the story? What choices do the characters make or respond to? What is accomplished or lost?

- ✓ Characters – Who are the players in the story? They are the ones who live out the story. I'm a firm believer in starting here with the development of your story. We'll get to this in a minute.

- ✓ Setting – Where does the story take place? Setting can be a character too. It adds tone, and theme, and can even be a protagonist. And if your novel is a historical book, that is a part of the setting as well.

Let's start with the Big Picture: **The Theme or the Story Question**

What is a Theme or Story Question?

Theme: Theme is the overall idea of a book or story. *The Hunt for Red October* is about betrayal and loyalty, about freedom. *Return to Me* is about eternal love and second chances. *Sweet Home Alabama* is about forgiveness and discovering your heart. But none of these really answer a question about life.

A **Story Question** asks *what if*? Most great stories start out with a "what if" question. *What if* a Russian nuclear submarine disappeared and you thought you knew why? (*The Hunt for Red October*) *What if* your wife died, and her heart was donated, and you fell in love with the new recipient without knowing it? (*Return to Me*) *What if* you returned home to divorce your first love, only to discover you still loved him? *(Sweet Home Alabama)*

A Story Question, however, isn't *just* the momentary "what if." A Story Question answers a deeper question for us all, a question of the heart or mind. It's the *great* "what if."

The Hunt for Red October: Can a man from one country know the heart and mind of a man from another?
Return to Me: Is it possible for a "heart" to pick its recipient and attract the same man twice?
Sweet Home Alabama: Can you find your soul mate at the age of six?

These are the questions that drive a story and resonate with readers, making them turn pages.

> *The most important thing in a work of art is that it should have a kind of focus, that is, there should be some place where all the rays meet or from which they issue.*
>
> **Leo Tolstoy**

So, how do you develop a Story Question?

Ask:
- ✓ What is my subject matter? Love, greed, betrayal, loyalty?

- ✓ What am I saying about my subject? Maybe I'm saying love doesn't end at death, or loyalty to self trumps loyalty to country.

Turn your statement into a question and make it specific to your character, and thus, to the reader.

Does love end at death, or is it possible to follow the "body" of your loved one, unknown to you, by a sort of cosmic fate? Is it possible to know someone through outside analysis, enough to predict their movements and decision?

The answer to these questions will be portrayed through the drama and the plot of your story. Your characters shouldn't have to explain your story at the end. They should be showing the answer.

Every author should identify their Story Question at some point in their story, and definitely before they pitch to an editor. Sometimes I don't discover my Story Question until half-way through writing the story, and then I have to go back and adjust everything. So I definitely encourage you to find your Story Question before you get too far into your manuscript. Print your Story Question out and post it on your computer. It will be essential when you develop your synopsis and query letter, so fix your Story Question firmly in your mind.

"You don't write because you want to say something; you write because you've got something to say."

F. Scott Fitzgerald

Your Turn:

What are some of your favorite movies and can you define their Story Question?

What is *your* novel's Story Question?

So now you what kind of book you're writing, and you know the Big Picture, or Story Question. However, regardless, of which genre you're writing, all plots have the same foundational elements. So, let's take a closer look at the basics of a plot.

THE BASIC PLOT

Because I'm a gal who loves lists, I've come up with an acrostic to help you keep your plot straight. And, hey, let's have a little fun and dance our way through discovery.

The Lindy Hop

Every book has a three-act structure, with the first being the introductory and set-up, the middle being the "guts" and the final act being the "glory," or Big Finale. Here's how it breaks down. I promise, we'll go through *all* these in more detail as we get deeper into Discovery.:

Act 1: Lindy Hop
- ✓ *Life or Normal World* – This is the world in which your character normally lives. Their challenges, their status quo. Sometimes this is a chapter long, maybe longer, although more and more, it's shortening to the first few pages. It gives us a glimpse of their regular life.
- ✓ *Inciting Incident* – Something happens. Some writing classes call it the trigger, or ignition. But it's the first blip in their world, big or small, that will change it and set them on the course of their journey.
- ✓ *Noble Quest* – The effect of theInciting Incident is to start a quest. In the case of an unpleasant Inciting Incident, the quest is to return to the normal world. In a positive Inciting Incident, the quest is to increase that pleasure. In either quest, the hero must recognize what's at stake. The higher the stakes, to person, family, community, country, or world, the bigger the story, the broader the reader base.

Act 2:
- ✓ *Disappointments* – These are the obstacles and conflicts the hero encounters; even positive events can rumple the advancement of the plot. It may be caused by a revelation of information, or because of a choice, or because of outside forces. But the Disappointment has to contain two elements:

  Unexpectedness – Don't foreshadow the surprise too much or you will disappoint your reader.

  Plausibility – It has to be in the bounds of credibility.

- ✓ *Y in the Road* – Or "What am I going to do now?" Every character reaches a point where they have to make a choice about their actions. Do they quit? Is it worth the cost? Do they go forward? Often, the best stories include two equally worthy choices, and the character is forced to choose between external goals and internal goals. (We'll get to this.) Their choice, however, will spark new conflicts, and at some point they reach the point of no return. A good Y in the Road must involve:

Consequences – A plot must allow for a character's choices, and then consequences for those choices. Preferably, the character's choice lands them in a worse situation and leads to their darkest point. We'll be talking about character desires, and how a character makes these choices later in the book.

Surprises – These come up as the character continues to make choices in the middle act of the story, each one testing their mettle more and more.

Act 3:

✓ *HELP!* Or *Climax* – This is the final challenge, the event that the book has been building to. The character's goal is usually in jeopardy, and everything they've worked for is at stake. There is *no hope*. This is the Black Moment, where it seems that it can't get any worse. Often a character's Epiphany occurs right before or right after the Climax. (We'll talk about Epiphanies in the Character section.)

✓ *Overhaul* -- This is the change that occurs in the character, something internal or external, something that redefines them, and something logical that is derived from the journey.

✓ *Perfect Ending Resolution* – The new status quo, the new normal. This is when the character reaches the goal. As you write, keep in mind there must be an end game, something definable to the reader, and the character.

A Note about the Hero's Journey: So, you're saying…Wait! What about Joseph Campbell and his famous *The Hero's Journey,* that is the foundation for all novels? *The Hero's Journey* is an expansion on this basic plot. So, let's get this nailed down first, and then we can move into advanced dance steps!

The Lindy Hop (or basic plot structure):

Life… Once Upon a Time
Inciting Incident… Something out of the ordinary happens
Noble Quest… Causing the protagonist to seek something
Disappointment… But things don't go as expected
Y in the Road… Forcing the protagonist to make a difficult decision
Help!… Which has consequences
Overhaul… The result in which is a change in status
Perfect Ending… And they all lived happily ever after (or didn't!)

Your Turn

Can you identify the Lindy Hop in your favorite book or movie?

Life:

Inciting Incident:

Noble Quest:

Disappointment:

Y in the Road:

Help!:

Overhaul:

Perfect Ending:

Now identify the Lindy Hop in *your* book. It's okay if you don't know all the specifics, or even if you get it wrong. What ideas might you have for any of these plot points?

Life:

Inciting Incident:

Noble Quest:

Disappointment:

Y in the Road:

Help!:

Overhaul:

Perfect Ending:

By the way: Later on, as you write your synopsis, I'll ask you to refer back to this exercise, and then go through the summary or synopsis of your story and identify (even, highlight!) each of these elements.

It's All about CHARACTER

Okay, we're on to Characters. Before you can put one word on to paper, you need to know *who* you are writing about. When you think of a novel, the first thing that comes to mind should be the main character in the story. After all, what would be a James Bond book without James Bond? Or a Clancy novel without Jack Ryan? Even if it's the plot that stands out in your mind, your plot needs to happen to *someone* for the reader to connect to the story. So, we're going to talk about creating that special someone you'll be spending the next three (or more) months with—at least in your mind!

But first, I want to identify a few terms for you so we're on the same page. You will be working with each of these as you flesh out your characters.

- ✓ **Goals** – All characters will have external and internal goals that drive them through the story.
- ✓ **Motivation** – This will be the something behind their goals that is compelling enough to produce in them a desire for change and a desire to interact with the plot choices.
- ✓ **Conflict** – These are the people, events, and issues that stand in the characters' way, internally or externally, to keep them from accomplishing their goals.

How does GMC (Goals, Motivation and Conflict) work in a character?

For example, let's say we have a character who has a goal to open a bookstore. She has invested every last cent into the bookstore, so if it doesn't succeed, she's a flop. Her external goal is to have a successful bookstore. Her internal goal is to fulfill her father's dream, which was, ironically, to own a bookstore. But this deeper goal can't be reached just by the act of opening the bookstore. Why? Because of her motivation. Her father died, and not just any death, but a death she caused. Her motivation is guilt. So her inner goal, driven by her motivation, is to atone for her role in her father's death. So what's the conflict?

She buys a rundown house to turn into a bookstore, but it's in serious need of repair. She isn't a great handygal, nor does she have a lot of extra money. She needs cheap labor, so she hires a handyman/drifter to help her. However, mishaps keep occurring that push her further and further away from her goals. Which leads her to believe that the handyman she hired is to blame. The conflict is the house, the handyman, and her feelings of failure.

Good conflict should push your character further and further from their goals, yet strengthen their motivation to push ahead.

Many, many people develop characters based simply on GMC. And that's okay. In the end, you should be able to succinctly say what your character's GMC is. However, getting there should be a more introspective process, which I think, in the long run, will help you in developing plot.

Creating Characters from the Inside Out:

Throw away the list!
When I began writing, I did what seemed logical—I filled out character lists. Answered hundreds of questions. But my characters still felt flat, and more than that, their actions, dialogue, and conflicts didn't seem to ring true. At the time, I was homeschooling, and as I looked at developing my children's self-esteem, it hit me. People reveal themselves from the inside out, based on how they see themselves, on the five elements of self-esteem:

- ✓ Identity
- ✓ Purpose
- ✓ Competence
- ✓ Security
- ✓ Belonging

When we begin with these elements, we can create three-dimensional characters and even develop a plot driven by these nearly breathing people.

Let's keep dancing through discovery with a WALTZ

Let's start with a quick overview:

1. ***Who Am I?*** Identity: How do I define myself?

   Identity helps you define:
   1. Your values
   2. Your greatest fears
   3. Your greatest dream

2. ***At All Costs?*** Purpose: What is my Noble Cause in life?

3. ***Let Me Do It!*** Competence: What am I good at? What do I rely on when I am overwhelmed?

4. ***Teddy Bear*** Security: Where do I go for safety? What do I do when life is falling apart?

5. ***Zone*** Belonging: Where do I fit in God's world? Where do I believe I belong?

All these components work together to make you a three-dimensional person. Let's see how they fit together in creating your character.

WHO?

Getting to the bottom of your character's motivations, values, deepest fears, and greatest dreams!

Who am I? How do I introduce myself? I have an identity—as a wife, a mother, an author By those three words, I've given you a glimpse into who I am, based on your understanding of what those words mean to you. Everyone has an identity, a way they describe themselves. Knowing how our character defines himself or herself will help us understand their motivations. This also helps us figure out what their greatest fears and dreams are, and gives us insight into crafting that Black Moment.

Let's take a character I mentioned before: author Tom Clancy's Jack Ryan—a CIA analyst rising in the ranks who hasn't had much field action. He's a family man who wants to keep the world safe and out of WW III. In the movie *Hunt for Red October* his greatest fear is misinterpreting the actions of a Russian sub commander, whose sub has gone AWOL, and accidentally igniting WWIII. His greatest dream is to be right—and gain access to this sub. His motivation is his family, keeping them safe.

Knowing a person's identity helps us define their goals, and also reveals the means we can use to destroy them.

Just for fun, let's create a character and walk him through his identity. We'll call him Joe the Drifter.

> *What kind of person defines himself as a drifter?*

Maybe someone who has a hard time putting down roots? Avoids commitment? Why?

- ✓   Maybe he grew up in a broken home?
- ✓   Maybe he had a commitment, a family, and saw it destroyed.
- ✓   How?
- ✓   Maybe something happened in the family.

Like what? Maybe a loss of a job, or what if it involved an unexpected pregnancy, a child with physical challenges? What if his parents had a child with special needs, and it was too much for his father, so he left them? What if his mother is left with raising Joe's brother by herself, and she struggles financially and emotionally with his care?

How has that shaped Joe? He's learned that families with children who have unexpected challenges might not stay together. What if that condition was genetic? That would make Joe iffy about a relationship and commitment. He'd be afraid of this same thing happening to him. It would keep him from settling in too deep. What other components go into being a drifter? Maybe Joe likes adventure and new challenges. Maybe he's good at fitting in, at solving problems, at being a temporary savior.

The key is to keep asking why, until you get to the underlying motivations of your character's identity.

Once you're there, it's not too hard to discover the three things that will drive your plot and give your character resonance.

Identity helps you define:

> Your character's values
> Your character's greatest fears
> Your character's greatest dream

Values: These are the things that Joe desires, whether he has them or not. They are the longings that drive his actions. For example, because of his past, Joe values trust and family. Although his trust in relationships was destroyed, he needs them, and he yearns for the family he lost.

Knowing your character's values makes for excellent internal conflict. And here's the key: Pitting a character's values against each other makes for great character angst. For example, let's take Joe: If his values are trust and family, then he's going to do what it takes to earn someone's trust, and value that. Likewise, he's going to protect the family he has—his mother and brother. But, what if those two values were pitted against each other? What if he had to sacrifice the trust of someone in order to protect his family? Or sacrifice his family to earn the trust of someone he cared about? Makes for good inner conflict.

It also leads to mannerisms and ancillary information. Like why Joe might carry a picture of his family in his glove compartment, or have a soft spot for kids, making him volunteer at a children's shelter. Perhaps, also, he'd be secretive about all this, not wanting people to know about him.

> ***Knowing your character's values and motivations helps you create inner conflict.***
>
> ***Discovering your character's greatest fear and greatest dream will help you define the external conflict.***

Let's return to Joe's identity: **Drifter**

Knowing his past and his motivations, what would be Joe's greatest fear? What if his greatest fear was to be in a relationship that went bad? And what if it went bad in the same way his parents' did—by having a child with special needs? That fear will keep him drifting, and out of relationships.

But will his greatest fear be greater that his greatest dream? His greatest dream also stems from his identity, and it is probably being a family again. What if his dream is to put his family back together, and even more, have someone love him more than his father did—someone who would stick by him even if the worst happened?

We now have components to begin creating our plot. Joe's motivation, Joe's values, Joe's greatest fear, Joe's greatest dream. But we need one more component before we can go on to plot building and creating conflict.

PURPOSE: At All Costs?

Donald Maas, in his book, *Writing the Breakout Novel*, would call this "Noble Cause." Every character has to have something inside of them that drives them—that makes us like them regardless of what they've done, or who they are.

~ In *The Fugitive*, it's the fact that Dr. Kimball saves the little boy in the hospital. He's a doctor at heart.

~ In *The Hunt for Red October*, it's that Ryan wants to prevent WWIII.

~ In Joe's case, the attempts he makes to put his family back together will make us like him. What if he is secretly doing everything he can to earn money to support his mother and his brother? What if, when he disappears and seems to drift, he's really visiting them and helping his mom?

If you haven't figured it out yet, I've been talking about *Happily Ever After*, my first book in the Deep Haven series. Joe's brother, Gabe, has Down syndrome, and Joe is in town to reconnect with his brother and earn his forgiveness. This is the Noble Cause behind the scenes that make us forgive Joe for being aloof and a drifter, and a seeming saboteur.

When looking for a Noble Cause, go back to your character's deepest desire. Joe wants a family. He wants to build that which his father destroyed. So Joe will spend his life protecting and caring for his brother. It's also that Noble Cause that makes Joe memorable. It causes him to do things like sacrifice himself for others, maybe go fishing with his brother, or adopt a stray dog.

The Noble Cause makes us fall in love with our hero or heroine, and puts them in our hearts.

Create Conflict they can't live with!

Conflict is what drives a story. We talked about inner conflict—that conflict between competing values. And we pinpointed the external conflict by determining our character's greatest dreams and greatest fears. Now, let's use all that to create some conflict. Conflict can come from many sources: other people, weather, events outside our control, bad choices we make. A good story is driven by a character's choices. And the story is enhanced by their Noble Cause and motivations. We want our characters to be frustrated and feel out of control. How do we do that? **Attack their competence!**

COMPETENCE: That Which You Do Well.

What is that one thing you fall back on as your strength? Can you organize, take charge of things? Can you re-varnish furniture? Can you write?

Let's go back to *The Fugitive*. What did Dr. Kimball do to solve his wife's murder? He went to a hospital and submerged himself in that life. He even momentarily broke out of his disguise to help someone who needed surgery. He counted on his competence to get him through.

The competence is where you can hurt your character the most. You've all heard that good plotting makes each situation worse. You accomplish this by taking away a character's competence, bit by bit.

Consider Joe in *Happily Ever After*. Joe is a handyman. He prides himself on being able to tackle any situation and fix whatever the problem is. But what if everything he does backfires, through his fault, or through no fault of his own?

- ✓ In *The Fugitive* when Dr. Kimball saves the little boy, suddenly the agent chasing him has a new lead on him, and he's trapped again, his end goal now thwarted.
- ✓ One of my favorite scenes in *The Hunt for Red October* is when submarine captain Markos Ramius, played by Sean Connery, turns to Ryan and says, "Oh, I've heard of the book you wrote. It's all wrong." Suddenly everything we've assumed about Ryan's competency is destroyed, and there's the question: Are they all in big trouble?
- ✓ For Joe, his efforts to help someone only leads to more trouble for them. Suddenly, even his identity as a drifter/handyman, the guy who can solve problems, the temporary savior, is shaken.

In the end, Joe's confidence needs to be completely destroyed, which is a great place for God to step in and do something incredible. *Destroying your character's competency also helps to build to your Black Moment.*

The Black Moment

That place in the book where everything hits a crisis, where internal and external conflicts come to a head. It's the climax of the book and can be the most powerful scene *if it's done right.*

Teddy Bear SECURITY

Where do you derive your security? Hopefully, for all of us, we derive our security in the strength of God and trusting in His love for us. But not everyone has that strength of faith. Most of us can admit that, when we are broadsided by life, not all of us go running to the Bible or prayer first.

Maybe you call your mother.

Or exercise. Or dive into the refrigerator. Or gather in your children.
Maybe you go home and curl up on the sofa with the Lifetime Channel. Or take long walks. Maybe some of us run from our problems, while others charge in like a bull and try to organize or control our way out of them.

> **What is your security?** Joe, the hero in *Happily Ever After*, has a history of leaving. Hitting the road when the going gets tough. He trusts only himself, and when life hits the skids, he finds his security by packing up and going in search of new beginnings, leaving the old dangling like threads. He's got a lot of loose ends.
>
> Defining your character's security blanket—the one he reaches for before he finds salvation or spiritual depth—will help you craft that climactic moment of choice, that "Aha!" moment where everything changes. At some point in the book, Joe has to confront the failures of his past. He has to make a choice: Will he continue to run, or will he stay planted? If he does decide to stay, it will change his identity. So, ask your character: When the going gets tough, what do you do?

Now, gather up the building blocks you have created.

Poor Joe

Motivation: His past makes him afraid of developing deep relationships.

Greatest Fear: That he will get into a relationship and it won't survive the challenges, especially the very possible one of a special-needs child.

Greatest Dream: To restore his family

Purpose: To be the caregiver his father wasn't and provide for his brother (while still not sacrificing his heart).

Competence: His handyman skills—only they aren't working. In fact, they're making the situation worse. Black Moment must come when there is no longer anything Joe can do to "save" the day except face his greatest fear. In Joe's case, that would be continuing a relationship that will only hurt him because he'll have to leave. This will cause the inner conflict: What if he has to sacrifice the trust of someone in order to protect his family? Or sacrifice his family to earn the trust of someone he cares about?

As I develop my plot, I want to draw my character deeper and deeper into trouble. I try and set it up with three "Trouble" points, leading to the final "Turning" point, and ending with the Happily Ever After that brings it full circle.

Here's how it works:

As you create your character, you know what his dream is. Now think of the things in his normal world that pull him away from his dream. We're going to start him in a place of **UnHappy.**

Hint of Trouble often happens in conjunction with the Inciting Incident—that event or decision that makes it seem he won't get his desire. Again, it's in the world of his competence, so as you figure it out, relate it personally to your character.

Trouble along the way are the "Disappointments" on your character's quest that push him further and further from his goal until he reaches that Y in the Road! I recommend at least three "Disappointments."

Big Trouble is the Black Moment, where there is no turning back, and no hope.

I also think through the **Happily Ever After** so I know what my ending will be.

How do you determine the "Trouble" your character will get in? Attack his competence! With each swipe at his competence, you now bring him further and further from his dream and purpose.

And when he reaches the Black Moment, his point of no return, he'll be facing his worst fears and be tempted to revert to security mode. He'll either grab the Teddy Bear, or choose to change.

In Dr. Kimball's case, he's been on his own so much, and his greatest fear is that no one will ever know the truth about his wife. Even more than his freedom, he values justice—he wants her murderer caught. So when the agent tracking him offers him this opportunity, he's faced with his greatest dream happening, or losing everything by betrayal. If he surrenders, he's risking his freedom, and facing his greatest fear: going to jail and never solving the crime. If he doesn't trust the agent, he's risking the dream that the murderer will come to justice.

You have to bring your character to this point of choice, where his competence is at an end, his identity is threatened, his security is calling him, and his purpose is dangled before him at great risk. Then it's time for your divine paradigm shift, which brings us to the Epiphany.

An **Epiphany** is that AHA! moment when your character suddenly realizes why he's on the journey. He realizes that what he's believed all his life, what's been driving him, is a lie. This is accompanied by a truth that unlocks possibilities to become a new person. It usually precedes a change in character, beliefs, or values.

THE ZONE, or Where do you belong?

If you're writing an inspirational book, there has to be a spiritual component to the plotting—God's handiwork woven throughout the plot.

I have a theory: Your hero needs to look inward to understand what holds him back from being the person he longs to be. This is true whether you're writing for the American Booksellers Association (ABA) or the Christian Booksellers Association (CBA).His journey is more about an inward change than an external change. Even the characters in the high-action stories—Frodo in *The Lord of the Rings* or Jason Bourne in *The Bourne Identity*—are at their heart about self-discovery of the hero.

If you're writing an inspirational novel, then God has brought your character to this point to bring him to some kind of wholeness. Up until now, your character has been largely egocentric, with the exception of the Noble Cause. Now, God brings him to this last step. Overwhelmed, at the Black Moment, ready to withdraw with his security blanket, he gets to see God reach out and save him.

Regardless of the kind of book you are writing, your character will start out in a place of dissonance, an unhappy place. Creating the Epiphany is all about moving your character from one place to the other, from the Dark to the Light.

Or, from the Lie he believes to the Truth. **One way I approach this is to ask**: What is the Lie that my character has believed? Often, it's something from his past that has made an impression on him and taught him a lesson, and he's lived his life by that set of rules, by the Lie ever since. If I discover this, I can then determine how he sees himself, and the ways he's imprisoned himself. And from there I can see the Truth that will set him free.

The thing is, if you've written the story right, in a way that the reader not only connects with your character, but also sees himself in that character's shoes, the Truth can extend from the pages into the reader's heart. It can minister, and change lives. In this paradigm shift, or the "Aha!" moment, your character sees that lesson that God has been teaching him.

So, let's put these five components together:

Again, poor Joe.

Who am I? (Identity): Drifter

At all Costs? (Purpose): To restore his family

Let Me Do It! (Competency): Problem Solver

Teddy Bear (Security): Flee to new beginnings

Zone (Belonging): Broken Family, from fatherless to Child of God

Now, as a writer, you know what needs to happen on Joe's journey. Take that germ of an idea, that setting or situation or Inciting Incident, and start Joe on his journey.

1. You need to establish his identity as a drifter, and along the way reveal his motivations. That's your backstory.

2. Then you have to remind us of his Noble Cause, his purpose in life. See him begin to fulfill that purpose he's set out to accomplish. Give him a taste of what that would feel like, and dangle his greatest dream in front of him.

3. Then you have to establish his competence.

   a. It's important to establish for the reader that he is, indeed, good at what he does. Like Jack Ryan knowing so much about his Russian captain, or Dr. Kimball tending his own wounds.

   b. Then continue to chip away at his competence until everything falls apart. Use "Trouble" to bring him closer to his greatest fears.

4. Finally, that Black moment occurs when his greatest fears are about to come true, that moment when he has to battle between his inner values and face the choice of reverting to security mode, or changing.

5. And this is where the divine paradigm shift comes in, that God-Aha! moment where he sees the light that changes him, makes him able to grow and, hopefully, reminds us that God is at work in our lives.

I know this is a lot to digest. So, I'm going to tell you a story that brings this all together: The Lindy Hop and the WALTZ, in three acts.

How do Plot and Characterization fit together?

Sally and the Dresser

LIFE

There once was a girl named Sally, who was a housewife. She and her husband and children moved to America from another country. They didn't have much money, but they decided to build a house. Now, Sally came from a very good family, and her mother had the nicest of houses. She filled her home with expensive things, teaching Sally the importance of creating a nice home. Sally was adopted, and more than anything, she wanted her mother to approve of her. She wanted to be like her beautiful, capable mother and provide a nice home, like the Proverbs 31 woman. She also wanted to be frugal, and to please her husband, who had her on a terribly thin furniture budget. In the past, Sally had dealt with frustration through "shopping therapy," sometimes overspending. Sally's inner values were approval and frugality. And her dream was creating a beautiful home without spending much money. Her greatest fear was wasting money. Her Noble Cause was to be the noble wife.

INCITING INCIDENT

Sally was very competent. She was a creative girl. She watched HG TV, liked *Design on a Dime*, and had recently created her very own ottoman with an old table, some varnish, foam, and scrap material. So, when she spotted a dresser at a garage sale, an idea formed. She would take it home, strip it, and transform the dresser into a thing of beauty that could house her table linens.

(THE STORY QUESTION: CAN SALLY BE THE PROVERBS 31 WOMAN? THE STAKES: HER FRUGAL AND HG TV REPUTATION, HER FAMILY'S BEAUTIFUL HOME)

NOBLE QUEST *(Ignition)*

Sally wrestled the dresser into the car, feeling some victory. Returning to town before returning home, she purchased what she felt she needed for the project, thrilled with the three hours she had to work on the dresser before she had to take her children to the doctor for their yearly physicals. She arrived home, finagled the dresser back out of the car onto the driveway, and began her project. Wanting her children to learn and grow from a new experience, she strongly suggested they assist her in the project. She tuned the car radio to a radio station and began to strip the dresser.

DISAPPOINTMENT 1

Soon fumes and children complaining of getting stain remover on their hands and clothing damped Sally's enthusiasm, but she began to see progress and the lovely sheen of wood. However, the stripping didn't proceed as quickly as she'd hoped, and two hours later, Sally had to interrupt the process and clean herself and her children up for their doctor's appointments. Getting into the car with plenty of time to spare, she congratulated herself on a pretty good job so far, but determined that she would finish the project alone when they returned home. Glancing at the darkening sky, she felt a sense of foreboding. But not to be deterred, and thankful that she'd made the doctor's appointments months in advance, well in time for school physicals, she attempted to start her car. Much to her dismay, the battery had died, with all the radio playing. *(Unexpected, yet plausible!)*

Y in the Road 1 *(WHAT IF: WILL SALLY'S HUSBAND BE ANGRY WITH HER IF SHE CALLS HIM? WILL SHE LOSE HIS RESPECT?)*

Frustration needled Sally as she returned inside to call her husband home from work to help jumpstart the car. Meanwhile, she phoned the annoyed doctor. Her husband was less than pleased with his interruption from work, and said little as he started the car. Sally and the children made it to the doctor's office a half-hour late, but were still able to have their physicals. Sally returned home, sent the children inside, and began to finish her project.

DISAPPOINTMENT 2

Sally found that she had underestimated the amount of materials she would need. She decided she would only refinish the top and the fronts of the drawers, yet she'd revarnish the entire piece. While she was painting on the varnish, she was horrified to see her husband coming home from work. Time had slipped away, and she hadn't put dinner on the table!

Y 2 *(WHAT IF IT RAINS? WHAT IF SHE PUTS OFF HIS DINNER?)*

Finishing her work quickly, Sally decided to run inside to fix hamburgers, leaving the dresser in the driveway, exposed to the elements.

DISAPPOINTMENT 3

Over dinner, her husband expressed concern at the cost of the project. Sally felt further discouraged when she returned outside three hours later and discovered that varnish made excellent glue for dragonfly wings. (Unexpected and plausible). Hundreds of dragonflies lay forever pinned to the surface of her beloved dresser, their legs wiggling in a horrific dance.

Y 3 *(WHAT IF SHE CAN'T GET THE DRAGONFLIES OFF? WHAT IF SHE HAS JUST WASTED ALL THAT MONEY?)*
With that image of torture in her mind, Sally went to bed . . .

HELP!

. . . Only to hear the rumble of thunder in the distance. With rain pelting the windows, and her project outside, Sally realized that she could do no more. She had failed. She would have to spend more money to fix the disaster she had created. Her husband was angry, her children's clothes were ruined, and Sally's frustration boiled over. Her values competed with each other: Did she choose beauty and her mother's approval, or frugality? Did she surrender the dream of a beautiful masterpiece, and would her greatest fears of wasting money pull her under? Did she turn to the credit card, and her old ways of dealing with problems? At that moment, she wondered, *What did God want?* Would she believe the lie that she would never be the Proverbs 31 woman, capable of taking care of her home and earning the esteem of others? Or did God's truth set her free to find her approval in Him?

OVERHAUL

The question drove her to her knees. And in the darkness, she heard God say, "Cast your burdens upon me." *(EPIPHANY)*

PERFECT ENDING

The next morning Sally discovered that the rain had washed away the dragonflies. And with the leftover varnish remover, she was able to smooth out the drops. She began to see the project with a new eye, and instead of a pristine piece of furniture, the dresser looked quaintly distressed. Not quite perfect, but beautiful it it's own right. Sorta like Sally.

The dresser now sits in her living room, its rustic appearance fitting perfectly into her décor. And without fail, guests comment on its beauty and originality. Sally simply smiles at her dream come true.

The End

Your Turn:

Okay, you're going to stop looking at other books and movies. Turn your focus inward. I want you to interview your character. Yes. Sit down, have a cup of coffee in hand, lock your door, and imagine your hero (or heroine) in your mind. You are the therapist. It's time to get to the bottom of things!

Basic Bio:
Name:
Age:
Profession:

Who are you? (Keep asking "Why?" until you get to their motivations and values.)

What would you would die for? (Noble Cause/Purpose)

What are you good at?

When the going gets tough, what do you do?

Spiritual Epiphany

What monumental event in your past shaped your beliefs today?

What is the Lie that you believe, and what Truth will set you free?

Now let your character off the couch and take some notes.

What is his greatest fear?

What is his greatest dream?

Gathering all your information, what could be a possible Black Moment for your hero?

Look at all you're discovering! Isn't this fun? Let's keep going!

A Few Pointers on Heroes vs. Heroines

How to Write a Heartthrob Hero

A great hero who leaps off the page and into our hearts—Every book has to have one! Think of your favorites: William Wallace in *Braveheart*, or maybe Robin of Loxley in *Robin Hood*? Maybe it's simpler: William Thacker, played by Hugh Grant, in *Notting Hill*. Whoever your favorite heroes are, they all have the same elements that make them heroic.

So, what are the elements of a winning hero?

Noble – Every hero has something to fight for. As Miracle Max says in *The Princess Bride,* "What you got here that's worth living for?" Wesley's answer? "True Love." Every hero should have something he believes in, something we find noble and true and worth believing in him, even when he acts like a cad to the woman he loves. Maybe it's a secret, or a wish, or a past mistake. It could be a dream, or something he's protecting the heroine from. But it needs to be strong enough for him to win the reader. Give your hero a Noble Cause!

Flawed – Our hero has to be less than perfect. There's something about him that makes him real. Maybe he has issues with recklessness, or perhaps he trusts too much and has gotten burned. Maybe he's jaded and mean on the outside (but of course tenderhearted on the inside). Some flaw is fixable, but that makes him less than perfect.

Fearful – Our hero has to have a fear. This fear must be deep—one that would keep him awake at night, or drive him to do stupid things, make stupid decisions. Sometimes a novel will start out with his fear being realized, and the result is so horrible we understand why he will run from it. A fear will build until the Black Moment, and make him human. The fear—and eventually his courage to face it—willcause us to love him.

No Wimps! – A hero has to have the courage to change. We don't like heroes that are stuck in their ways, that don't see their need for change, who are unwilling to take up the sword and fight the battle. Why is *The Matrix* so popular? Because it's about an ordinary guy who dared to reach out with his gut and fight for something real and better. He can be reluctant, for sure, but in the end, he has to see the greater good of going into battle for what he wants (and ultimately, for the woman he wants).

Give your hero these four qualities, putting them with a winning heroine (see matching sidebar on creating heroines!), and they'll be loved by readers far and wide!

How to Create Heroines Who Can Take Care of Themselves! (But they still want a good man!)

I used to hate romances. Why? Because I didn't respect a woman who had to have a man save her. But I did respect a woman who allowed a man into her life to make her better, stronger, more noble, more complete.

Which is why, probably, all the heroines in my books are strong women: CIA agents, and K-9 Handlers, and bush pilots, and fire chiefs.

But for all the toughness of my heroine, she needs a good man. So what makes a strong heroine?

Goal – Give her a measurable goal. Both your hero and heroine need to have a goal, but it's essential for your heroine. She needs to be proactive, and fight for something she believes in. We want to get on board with her cause, and fight the fight with her. Making her proactive and strong makes her noble—and a winner in our book.

Confidence – Give her a sense of self that is confident, despite her flaws. It's easy for a heroine to have flaws—mostly because we write about ourselves, and we all have flaws. So you need to work at putting confidence into your heroine, and giving her something she's good at, that makes us applaud her.

Fear – Give her a fear, something realistic and based on something in her past. Don't make it about "being single." And make her fear deep, something the hero has to figure out, even pry out of her. Having a realistic fear is something that will create sympathy in your reader, and put her in the heroine's shoes.

Flaw – Give her a flaw, one that she can start to overcome because of the hero. It doesn't have to be a huge flaw. Maybe it's a tendency to run away from her problems, or better, a tendency to push men out of her life. As she gets to know the hero, he can help her overcome these flaws and grow stronger.

Beauty – Give her a special kind of beauty, both inner and outer, that only the hero can see/love. Something special, that's only hers. Maybe it's her eyes, but also the way that she can look right through him and see what he needs. Or maybe it's her patience. Maybe it's her strength to see the good, or believe in the good.

These five elements will create a heroine worthy of the hero, who will fight for her heart!

Premise! What's It All About?

So, you know what kind of story you're going to write, and you know who it's about. Generally, you know the Black Moment, and the Epiphany, and some of the bad "Trouble" that will happen along the way. Hopefully your story is starting to come alive, ideas poking you in the middle of the night, or scenes flashing before your eyes.

But you're still discovering the story, so hold back, fellow writer . . . you're nearly ready to write! The next two chapters work together to help you get to that first page, so you may need to go back and forth as you develop your story. But the first thing you need to know is: What is your story about?

Think back to when we were packing for our writing journey. What are you going to take? Kind of hard to know whether to pack a swimsuit or a ski outfit if you don't know where you're going. Are you hiking the Himalayas? Going on a beach vacation in Cancun? Skiing in Vermont? How about a canoe trip in Minnesota?

Before you take your first step, you need to know what your journey is going to look like. And that means knowing your premise.

> A **premise** is a two to five sentence blurb of your story. It's zeroing in on the *most* important elements of your book: the stakes, the fears, the dreams, the theme, the plot, and the main players.

You'll use your premise to grab an editor's attention in your query letter or to pitch your book at a conference. But for now, you'll paste a copy of your premise above your computer. This will be a guidepost for your journey, so you want to make the premise compelling, exciting, and interesting.

The premise boils down to the most important aspects of your story, the biggest interest catcher—all in one short paragraph.

Here's a sample premise from my book *Happily Ever After*:

Mona Reynolds longs for two things: forgiveness, and Jonah, the hero from her favorite book. But getting either is about as likely as her father rising from the dead.

Tells you a lot, right? (I hope!) It tells you that Mona likes to read, that her father died, and that there's no way she's going to be forgiven. The theme of the book is forgiveness, and the story is about Mona getting her dream man. (That's a plug to read *Happily Ever After*, if you didn't recognize it!) The premise tells the editor just what the conflicts are, and what the book's theme is.

Here's the premise from *Tying the Knot*. If you aren't familiar with either of these books, go to my Web site (www.susanmaywarren.com). There are premises and first chapters there, under the "writing" link.

Noah Standing Bear has a knack for being in the right place at the right time. But when he sees a woman gunned down, can he help her find healing? Worse, when it happens again, what will it cost him to save her?

And here's the premise from *The Sovereign's Daughter*:

Royal daughter Oksana can't believe her father entrusted her life to a lowly peasant. Peace-loving Mennonite merchant Anton Klassen is paralyzed by his charge—especially when he falls in love with her. Can two people from different lives find a way to protect Russia's most valuable secret?

Let's play a little game. Can you guess what movies these premises are from?

A.   She just wants to prove she can be a Pulitzer-prize winning writer. He wants to be the top executive at his ad agency. But when two high achievers are thrown together to achieve their own goals, they just might discover that falling in love is the greatest prize of all.

B.   She gave up on her future, believing her true love dead, and agreed to marry a king. But when her fiancé returns, ready to fight for her, can she believe in love, even when it seems the past has repeated itself? And will he be a man of his word—even beyond the grave?

Those two premises focused on the romance part of the story. Let's try one without romance:

C.   He believes he can prevent war with his information about a Soviet secret. But what if he's wrong? What if, in fact, he instead pulls the trigger on WWIII? Just how far will one man's beliefs take him . . . and the rest of the world?

Answers:
A: *How to Lose a Guy in 10 days*
B: *The Princess Bride*
C: *The Hunt for Red October* (Of course!)

Your Turn:

Pick your favorite movie(s) and see if you can create a premise.

Crafting Your Premise in Six Easy Steps!

I love crafting a premise. It's one of the first things I do after I get a story in my head. With my premise as my guide, I know where the story is headed, the main themes, and the stakes. For those writers who are Seat of the Pants plotters (SOTPs), you can still do this. You don't have to nail down every scene and nuance right now. But I'll bet you have in your head the theme, the characters, and what the story is about. That's all you need to craft a great premise.

In a premise I like to start out with the **highest stakes**, the point at which the editor or reader might care about the outcome. I boil down the action to the most important, the **climax,** wind it together with the hero's and the heroine's deepest fears or needs (revealing the **Black Moment**), and ask an emotion question that will propel the editor to further reading. (Some would call that the **Story Question**.) But how do you pull all these elements together into something that pops, yet encapsulates the story?

Six Easy Steps to Creating a Premise

> **Step One:** Name your character, and their significance. For example, if the story is about a veterinarian, and her job is crucial to the story, then her occupation should be named. If she's a veterinarian who is returning home after being gone for years, and the story is about her return, then you might want to identify her as the town prodigal. If it's about a veterinarian who is returning to her mother's funeral, you might want to call her a wayward daughter. Use whatever moniker that describes your character and their most important role in the story.

> **Step Two:** Identify your character's goals for the story. Goals could be their greatest dream, or just the plot goals, but the reader must know what the story is about. For a romance, often the premise focuses on love, and finding the ideal mate. For a suspense, it's about life and limb, and saving those we love. For a mystery, it's about following the clues and solving the murder. Find that thing that is most important to the character.

Let's consider the veterinarian. Let's say she is returning home to her mother's funeral—only to discover her mother was murdered.

Wayward daughter Rachel Higgins wishes she hadn't waited until her mother died to return to Anytown, FL. If only she'd been here, maybe she could have stopped her murder. Now, she's on the trail of the culprit . . . and discovering that the killer has turned his sights on her.

Okay, that's rough. But it's a start. Let's keep moving.

> **Step Three:** Throw in the conflict. Often, it's the hero, and you need to return to Step One to identify him, with a brief stopover at Step Two to also collect his goals.

Wayward daughter Rachel Higgins wishes that she hadn't waited until her mother died to return to Anytown, FL. If only she'd been here, maybe she could have stopped her murder. Now, she's on the trail of the culprit . . . and discovering that the killer has turned his sights on her. The last thing Detective Brett Collins needs is a grieving daughter to tell him how to do his –job—a job he's close to losing, thanks to a fear that's plagued him ever since he was shot.

> **Step Four:** Now, you want to sift through all the stakes in the story, all those pivotal events, all those themes, and find the most compelling. Frame it in a statement of conflicting values, or goals.

Wayward daughter Rachel Higgins wishes that she hadn't waited until her mother died to return to Anytown, FL. If only she'd been here, maybe she could have stopped her murder. She'll stop at nothing to find her mother's killer. The last thing Detective Brett Collins needs is a grieving daughter to tell him how to do his –job—a job he's close to losing, thanks to a fear that's plagued him ever since he was shot. But Rachel is a good sleuth—good enough to land her in the killer's sights, and Brett must choose between protecting her, and catching the murderer.

(Notice that I took out the sentence: *Now, she's on the trail of the culprit . . . and discovering that the killer has turned his sights on her*. I decided I wanted to use the word "sights" later to ramp up the tension in the last line. I also don't like the use of the word "stop" twice in the beginning. I'll change that later when I polish the premise.)

> **Step Five:** Now we're onto the last line, the Story Question, or the ominous statement. I could probably stop the premise where it is right now, because there is enough information to know what is at stake. However, because it is also a romance, I'll add a line to focus the theme.

Wayward daughter Rachel Higgins wishes that she hadn't waited until her mother died to return to Anytown, FL. If only she'd been here, maybe she could have stopped her murder. She'll stop at nothing to find her mother's killer. The last thing Detective Brett Collins needs is a grieving daughter to tell him how to do his –job—a job he's close to losing, thanks to a fear that's plagued him ever since he was shot. But Rachel is a good sleuth—good enough to land her in the killer's sights, and Brett must choose between protecting her, and catching the murderer. But worse than putting hislife on the line is knowing that he just might lose his heart.

That's still rough. But we'll fix it:

> **Step Six:** Using strong, colorful words to add to the theme and tone of the premise.

> **If only wayward daughter Rachel Higgins had returned home sooner, her mother might still be alive. Now, Rachel's last act of atonement will be finding**

her killer. The last thing Detective Brett Collins needs is a desperate victim derailing his investigation—especially since his job is at stake. He's been off his game ever since he was shot. Rachel is a good sleuth, —however—good enough to land her in the killer's sights. Brett must choose between protecting her, and catching the murderer. And when it all goes south, the biggest casualty of all just might be his heart.

I used some pop words to give it energy: atonement, desperate, killer's sights, casualty. Finding words that shape the premise will give your entire story color.

Those are the basic steps to crafting a premise! Now, that wasn't so hard, was it?

Premise Steps: Recap

Step One: Name your character, and their significance.
Step Two: Identify their goals for the story.
Step Three: Throw in the conflict.
Step Four: Find the highest stakes.
Step Five: State the story question.
Step Six: Use strong, colorful words to ramp up the tension and hone the theme.

Premise Examples: Sometimes it's easier to see an example of what you're trying to accomplish. Here are a couple of premises from fellow *My Book Therapy* Voices who allowed me to work on their blurbs. Let's examine how they break down.

Premise 1: Women's Fiction

It's the Roaring Twenties and Evie Kimball bucks a life of wealth and privilege for big dreams and true love. Naively believing she can have it all, Evie leaves her true love waiting in the wings and sets off for the bright lights of Broadway. As the Great Depression envelopes New York, Evie returns home, ready to make amends with the one she left behind. But love doesn't wait forever, and Evie finds a hopelessness greater than that which the loss of fame and fortune has already brought her. Eventually, Evie reclaims some semblance of the good life and focuses on raising her family, but secrets and unforgiveness are always there threatening her happiness and tearing apart her family. So, on the eve of her one hundredth birthday celebration, Evie sets about to break the legacy of despair that has plagued her family for three generations.

I love Roaring Twenties books! And this one sounds very epic. It also sounds like the story might start on her 100th birthday, and we got a great introductory blurb about her backstory. Let's go through the six steps and see what we can do to restructure this premise a bit:

> Step One – Evie Kimball – socialite, heiress, dreamer, aspiring actress. Probably the actress characterization is the strongest in this lineup.

> Step Two – She dreams of being an actress, and naively believes true love will wait.

> Step Three – Conflict – the Great Depression, and her true love doesn't wait. There is no hero point of view (POV) here.

> Step Four – Evie marries someone else, and secrets and unforgiveness threaten to tear about her family's happiness

> Step Five – Can she learn to forgive before it's too late?

> Step Six – dazzled, empty, broken, sweeping. These words add just a bit of color to the premise.

One of the interesting elements is the legacy of despair. I think that is an angle that could really be explored.

Aspiring actress Evie Kimball is dazzled by the bright lights of Broadway. Believing her true love will wait, she heads to New York, only to return years later to her hometown, empty and broken, thanks to the sweeping despair of the Great Depression. Worse, her love has chosen another—something she can't forgive. Despite the fact that she marries, and has a family, she seems destined to live a life of brokenheartedness, like her mother, and grandmother before her. Will Evie learn, before it's too late, how to forgive?

I left out the 100-year-old birthday, because maybe that's not the crux of the story, and I brought in the legacy of despair. I also put the premise in active voice, which adds energy, and added some punch words.

Premise 2: A Regency!

Because of the lecherous bailiff who once accosted her, Annabel is afraid of men and horrified at the thought of marrying. Instead, she dreams of becoming a nun and of one day being allowed to read the Holy Writ. When her family's debts cause her to become indentured to wealthy Lord Ranulf, all hope seems lost.

Lord Ranulf is shocked by his feelings for his new servant. After being mauled and disfigured by a wolf at age sixteen, no one as beautiful as Annabel could want him. Didn't his dead wife prove that? When a murder in his village hangs a cloud of suspicion over Lord Ranulf, his silence will protect Annabel, but may cost him his life.

Step One – Annabel – Afraid of men, abused, wounded, devout, indentured.

Step Two – She dreams of being a nun and reading the Bible, but she isn't free.

Step Three – Lord Ranulf -- Disfigured and widowed. He is in love with his servant girl. He could have her if he wanted her, but true love demands that he grant her dreams.

Step Four – In order to protect her, Ranulf must take the blame for a murder he didn't commit.

Step Five – Will he, for the sake of love, lose his life, as well as his heart?

Step Six – hide, fallen, buy, sacrifice. These words give the feeling of indentured servanthood and nunneries.

All indentured servant Annabel St. Francis* wants to do is become a nun. After all, that will not only allow her to her hide herself away, reading the Holy Writ, but she'll never again be hurt by a man like the lecherous bailiff. Widower Lord Ranulf can't believe he's fallen for his servant—especially since he knows she can never love someone as disfigured as he. When tragedy strikes in his village and the locals accuse him of murder, his silence may buy Annabel the freedom she longs for. Just how much should he sacrifice in the name of love?

(*I took liberties with her last name.)Not knowing the author's intent—if they fall in love or not—I chose to craft this premise as one-sided romance. If you wanted to make it more traditional, the last line could be:

And when Annabel discovers his plan to free her, will her heart finally find a voice? (Or something to suggest she's in love with him too.)

So, break your idea down into six clean steps and craft your premise. If that feels too hard for you, then go onto the Inciting Incident, and come back to hone your premise after you've figured out where the book starts. You're still just discovering, so all of this is still a gray area, easy to shift around until it becomes what you envision.

Your Turn:

Write a loose paragraph about your story, whatever comes to mind.
(Think about your character, the Black Moment, the Epiphany, and what's at stake.)

Now, step by step, pull out your premise:

Step One: Character identity

Step Two: Goals

Step Three: Conflict

Step Four: Stakes

Step Five: Story Question

Step Six: Powerful words

Now **recast your premise** with the powerful words you've chosen. Write it on an index card and post it over your computer. Memorize it. When someone asks what your novel is about, tell them!

The Inciting Incident

Where do you start? Well, there your poor hero is . . . at home, chopping wood, lighting the home fires, and suddenly . . . *what*? What happens?

This is the Inciting Incident in your book! That moment when everything changes for your hero! The start of his journey.

The Inciting Incident is the event, moment of truth, issue, problem, quandary—whatever— that sends your hero (or heroine) on the story journey and often sets up the overall Story Question that the protagonist seeks to answer.

> *What are some popular Inciting Incidents?*
>
> ***Air Force One*** – Easy, huh? When the bad guys take over the plane. Or maybe not. How about when the security detail is killed? Go further back. It's when their Russian leader is captured and sentenced to die. For our hero, played by Harrison Ford, the Inciting Incident is when the bad guys take over Air Force One. And that's where the action really begins Everything before that is Normal World or Life. Remember your Lindy Hop?
>
> How about ***The Fellowship of the Ring***? Is it when Frodo runs away with the ring? Nope. It's when Bilbo puts it on and vanishes at his birthday party—and alerts the Nasgould to his presence.
>
> How about ***Return to Me***? Is it when Grace gets her new heart? Maybe for her, but Bob's Inciting Incident is when he meets her in the restaurant. Everything before that is backstory. So, for your characters you need to ask: What will jumpstart their journey?

I love the magic of a good Inciting Incident—that moment when everything goes haywire— or at least hints at going haywire—in our hero's journey. Sometimes it's an earthquake of epic proportions. Other times, it's just a 2.5 on the Richter scale.But regardless of the strength of the event, the Inciting Incident delivery demands an exquisite balance of **delicacy** and **resonance.**

Delicacy and Resonance?

Delicacy in the Inciting Incident doesn't mean a light touch.It means treading lightly through backstory, digging up only that which is most pertinent. It's so easy for an author to want to load in all the significant life events of the hero that have led up to this moment. Why, when he sees the red car parked in front of his mother's house, he realizes that his father has returned from years on the run. Or why, when our hero wakes up after being beaten up and left in an alley, he knows he wasn't just mugged. Yes, we as the reader need to know why these details matter, but light touches are the key when inserting back story.

I'm going to give you an example in just a moment from one of my books, but let's talk about Resonance for a moment.

Resonanceis *meaning*. We want to know how this event fits into the Story Quesstion, as well as the past. We also want to understand what the next step is for the character. However, we need to keep it free from melodrama. The reader wants to see the event, yet they don't know the character well enough for heavy interpretation.

So, how do we balance Delicacy and Resonance in our Inciting Incident? Answer: By keeping the backstory from stalling the –action—and keeping the action at the forefront.

Here's a scene from my book *Escape to Morning*. It's a romantic suspense, so I wanted to start right in the action. But I try to give you enough information to know that Will isn't who he seems. We don't need to know all of Will's past—just that he's trying to save his friend's life, that he was momentarily thrown by news from his past, and perhaps also that there's more at stake than just a reporter getting beat up in the woods.

Reporter Will Masterson didn't have time to be right. Time to prove that the men who'd hijacked him and hauled him into the forest to express their displeasure at his recent op-ed piece weren't actually disgruntled rednecks, but rather international terrorists. Because, the lie that had just saved Will Masterson's hide, the lie perpetuated by the boys toting 0.22s and wearing work boots was the only thing standing between undercover Homeland Security agent Simon Rouss and his brutal murder.

Which would only be the first in a hundred, maybe thousand murders by the terrorist cell hiding in the northern Minnesota woods.

Please, God, be on my side today. Will raced down the two-lane rutted forest service road, cursing his stupidity, wincing at a few new souvenir bruises. Blood dribbled from his nose, into his mouth. He should have known his sympathetic commentaries in the Moose Bend Journal toward the recent immigrants flooding over the Canadian border would have drawn blood with the locals. Blood that would hopefully protect Simon as he embedded deeper in the terrorist cell in the hills.

If only Will hadn't been ambushed by the double-edged sword sitting in his P.O. Box. A letter from Bonnie. He'd opened it, and the words knifed him through the chest.

Bonnie Strong and Paul Moore invite you to a celebration of life and love in our Lord Jesus Christ.

He should have dropped the invitation to his floorboard and crushed it under his foot. Instead, he'd let his grief, his failures, rush over him and blind him to the three hillbillies laying in wait like a nest of South Dakotan rattlers.

A year of undercover work, of slinking around this hick town in northern Minnesota, praying for a way to destroy the Hayat cell, and it all had to come to a head the same day his mistakes rose from the past to haunt him.

Sorry Lew.
Tell Bonnie and the girls I love them. Lew's words, hovering in the back of Will's mind could still turn his throat raw. And, if Simon bought it, Will would be sending yet another letter home to the wife and loved ones.

Soldiers like Lew and Simon, like himself, had no business getting married.

Will's breath razored inside his lungs. A branch clipped him and ruts bit into his thin loafers as he ran, sweat lining his spine. Overhead, the sky mirrored his despair in the pallor of gray, the clouds heavy with tears. How long had he been unconscious after they'd thrown him off the four-wheeler?

Better question – how much did they guess about his alliance with Simon? Obviously, the good ol' boys who snatched him as he'd sat in his truck, waiting for his contact and regretting his choices, knew Will's habits. Simon's habits. They'd found them, despite the fact that he and Simon had picked the backwoods gravel pit for its remoteness. But please, please, let them believe Will's lies . . . which would mean maybe Simon's cover hadn't been blown.

Maybe there wouldn't be another unnamed star embedded in the wall of honor at Langley.

Hopefully you see the setting, along with the emotion of panic, as well as regret in the backstory. From here, the story takes off into action, and we don't return to Lew's story (and how it fits into Will's motivation) until a few more chapters. However, we do know that Lew was a soldier, and that Will had to send his letter home, which makes Will sympathetic, as well as motivated to make sure it doesn't happen again. And, hopefully it has raised questions (e.g., who is Lew, what does the invitation from Bonnie have to do with the story, and what is Will's mission?) In the middle of the Inciting Incident, the last thing we want is a long, drawn-out history lesson. However, without some Resonance, we don't understand the motivation.

Think of backstory like a speed bump. It hiccups the reader's forward motion. As you're writing your scene, ask yourself, on every line;Have I bogged down the action? Here's a trick I try: After I've written the scene, I go through and ask myself if the reader need to know this. Can I take this line out? Can I say this more succinctly, with active verbs, in deeper POV that moves the story? And if I have to use backstory, I try to keep it to two lines at a time.

Okay, great, I have Delicacy and Resonance,but again, how ***do I start the story?***

Okay, okay . . . the answer? ***Start with a Big BANG!***

Let's see, over the past hour I've loaded the dishwasher, checked my e-mail, fed the dog, checked my e-mail, browned hamburger, checked my e-mail, made rice, searched for chocolate (none!), again checked e-mail . . . .

But see, I'm working. *Really.* What I'm doing is searching for my hero's Inciting Incident. I know what has to happen later on in the scene, what I hope to accomplish, but I need something powerful, something to really pinpoint how he's feeling at this very moment, to give the reader a glimpse into his world, and offer enough of a motivation to undergird his next step.

What I need is a BANG!! to get his (and my) attention.

How do you determine how and when to start your story? Do you start it on a calm day, set the scene, and then hit him with a BANG? Or, do you start him in mid-run, as he's being chased down the street? Or, should you start *after* the Inciting Incident, when he's trying to figure out what to do? And, do you start with something physical, or something emotional? Bad newsor bad event?

Here are the determinations that go into choosing my Inciting Incidents, and starting with a BANG!: Believability, Action, Need, Genre.

The Big BANG:

Believability – Do you need to build sympathy for your character before the Inciting Incident will have an impact on the reader? How understandable will your Inciting Incident be without background?

I recently saw the intriguing movie, *Jumper*. Because of the bizarre phenomenon that happens to the main character (his ability to jump through space), the viewer is given background to the story before he actually jumps, so we understand exactly what his skill is. Also, sympathy for the character is built before the actual Inciting Incident occurs so we understand why, when he jumps, he behaves so badly. These two elements—backstory and sympathy—are essential to our understanding of the hero.

Even longer is the wait for the Inciting Incident in Jodie Foster's vigilante movie, *The Brave One*. We need to care about her and her fiancé before the Inciting Incident has its intended impact, and result (to cause a normal person to become a vigilante).

However, the Inciting Incident in *Fools Gold* takes place immediately: the main character's boat sinks while he's searching for treasure. We don't have to know his character to feel sympathy for a guy whose boat sinks.

How believable and universal your Inciting Incident is determines how much character sympathy you need to build before it impacts your reader.

Action – Generally, the higher the action, the closer it should be to the beginning of the book. If you have high action, but it takes a while for the story to build to it, then you are wasting precious pages. In my book *In Sheep's Clothing*, the actual Inciting Incident didn't start until chapter two! Yes, I know! So I solved that by clipping out that scene and putting it into the prologue, and then starting the story twenty-four hours earlier in chapter one.

Then, when I got to chapter two and that scene, I told it from a different point of view, thus making it just as interesting. If, however, you have a slower, less active Inciting Incident, you may have to build in the impact (by focusing on characterization) of the Inciting Incident in order for it have resonance.

>**Need** – All stories are, to some extent, about a character's emotional journey. The character starts out with a need. What can you build into that Inciting Incident that reveals that need? For example, in my Inciting Incident for *Taming Rafe*, I develop his need to impress his family, and thus, the reason why he rides the bull even when he feels something is wrong. In *Get Cozy, Josey* (my third first-person funny book about Russian missionary Josey and her adventures), Josey's need is for a house with a backyard for her children. To meet her need, she agrees to go camping with her husband so he'll move back to America. Discovering your hero's need will help you determine what kind of Inciting Incident to put into the story.

>**Genre** – Certain genres demand different Inciting Incidents. First, keep in mind that *every* hero's journey starts in Life/Normal World. It starts with a glimpse of what his normal life is like, what his normal activities are, what his normal motivations and goals are. However, where you work that normalcy in differs by genre. For example, fantasy requires just a bit more setting (or storyworld, which we'll get to soon, I promise!) set up, a little more *normal* life for a character. A suspense, however, often starts with some high-action example of what is at stake, and then flows into normal. A romance might start at a point where the heroine meets the hero, and then spiral back to her normal day, or might even have a mix of normalcy inside the Inciting Incident, so that we don't even realize that it's the blip (or bloke) that will change her world. Look at other books in your chosen genre—where does the Inciting Incident occur? Page one? Three? Five? Ten? This is a good guide to how you might structure your book.

Every Inciting Incident will be specific to your book and your character, but determining how and when to put it in the book takes careful consideration of your BANG.

Your Turn:

Time to brainstorm your Inciting Incident!

What **Believable** Incident could occur in your hero's home world? How much sympathy do you need to build for your character to have the reader care that he's facing this incident?

What **Actions** could he take, or have happen to him?

What is (are) your character's primary **Needs**?

What **Genre** are you writing in? Look at your pile of genre books and read the first chapter, or at least the first page of three of them. What happens? Does this churn up any ideas for your hero?

Finally, what backstory elements do you need to include in order to give the Inciting Incident **Delicacy and Resonance**?

Okay, so you know *where* to place the Inciting Incident. The next question is *how*? (Of course, I have a few tricks for you!)

The Six Elements to an Inciting Incident!

What do all Inciting Incidents have in common? In the upcoming **CREATE** section, we'll be talking about the nuts and bolts of a **HOOK**, and we'll delve more deeply into many of these elements. It's important for you to start thinking about them as you craft your Inciting Incident.

> **Sympathy**
> **Stakes**
> **Motivation**
> **Desires**
> **Fears**
> **Action words**

Let's take a closer look:

1. Sympathy – Ask yourself: What situation can I put my hero in that would make my audience feel for him? What collective experience or feeling can I touch on that makes him instantly identifiable and creates sympathy in the reader? In *Nothing But Trouble*, a mystery featuring PJ Sugar, an amateur private investigator. PJ's Inciting Incident is returning to her hometown, and ending up fulfilling the prophecy of everyone who wants to see her fail. Because most of us have been in a situation where we've felt condemned by everyone around us, we can sympathize with PJ as I open the book with her in that very situation.

2. Stakes – We've talked about stakes for your story. How can you hint about them in your first scene? In the scene in the last chapter, from *Escape to Morning,* the stakes were all about saving Will's friend (an undercover agent) from being killed, and even saving America from terrorists. You don't have to explain everything. Asimple one-sentence hint of what is at stake will do the trick. But it should be something the reader will care about.

3. Motivation or Values – We need to know what about this situation motivates your hero to move to the next step in the journey. Returning to Will's scene in *Escape to Morning,* his motivation is the death of his friend, Lew. We could also substitute a hint of his values for motivation, because it is our values that drive our actions.

4. Desires – What does our hero care about, long for, dream of, that is at stake? Sometimes, in an Inciting Incident, I offer a hint of his dreams, only to then yank them away. But I want him to know (and the reader to know) what he has to live for. Often, I work this into the last part of the Inciting Incident, and often it's ever so subtle, but enough to know what the hero cares about. In the Inciting Incident in *TamingRafe*, we see Rafe inviting his pal Manuel's family to the big bull riding event, and we see that he is longing to have Manuel's life—a wife, a family, and the admiration in his son's eyes.

5. Fears – What is your hero deeply afraid of? Again, this is subtle, but it helps us to know him. For example, in Will's case, he's afraid that he won't be able to save his fellow agent. In PJ's case (my mystery heroine) it's that she'll forever be the failure/laughingstock of her town. One of the best Inciting Incident I've ever seen is in a Bruce Willis movie called *The Hostage.* (It's pretty violent, so don't feel like you need to run out and get it. I'll tell you the Inciting Incident here). Bruce is a hostage negotiator, and in the beginning of the movie, he is negotiating the release of a little boy. He fails in his negotiation, and the little boy is killed. This destroys Bruce, and he drops out of negotiation work. The thing is, his greatest fear is failing at negotiation, and having a child caught in the crossfire. In the first scene, we get a cemented picture of that, and it's used to great advantage when his own family is taken hostage. Hint at their greatest fears, and it will not only deepen your character, but give you something to work with in the plot.

6. Action words – The Inciting Incident has to be more than an event. You are trying to entice your reader to stick with the story. So you must "woo them with your words." Use vivid descriptions, and active, strong verbs. Pick the right words to convey mood, and give the scene texture. You want the words to reach out and pull your reader in, and not let go.

Now, before you say, "*What*? I can't possibly put all that into an Inciting Incident!" Yes, you can! In fact, you have probably already done this, without realizing it.

Here's an idea: First, write a rough draft of your scene, based on the last section's discovery notes. Now, take a highlighter (every author should be armed with an arsenal of different colors!) and go through your Inciting Incident, highlighting the six different elements of an Inciting Incident. You'll be surprised at what's there. And if it's not, you now know what to add.

I can't stress enough the importance of taking your time to craft the perfect Inciting Incident. It'll be your agent's, your editor's, and your reader's first introduction to your character, your plot, your theme, and your voice. Take the time to write it well.

Your Turn

Whether you've written your Inciting Incident or not, take the time to identify the six elements that will make it powerful.

What sympathetic situation is your character in?

What's at stake—in this scene, and in the book?

What are your hero's values, and what motivations do they lead to?

What are your hero's desires? His fears? And how can you use them to build tension in the scene?

Now, go through your scene and replace all the passive verbs with strong, action verbs.

Putting it all together: Your Plotting Roadmap

When I have my character, my Premise, my Inciting Incident, and my Black Moment all ironed out, it's time to put together the framework of the journey. I want to see the big picture, note the pit stops, the high points, the Black Moment, and the happy ending. Like being on a journey, I might not know all the discoveries I'll make on the way, but at least I'll know what direction I'm travelling.

Let's briefly revisit the Lindy Hop.

> Life
>
> Inciting Incident
>
> Noble Quest
>
> Disappointment 1, Y in the Road
>
> Disappointment 2, Y in the Road
>
> Disappointment 3
>
> Help! – Point of No Return
>
> Overhaul
>
> Perfect Ending!

It's a great start because know the basic moves now. But we need just a bit more shine to the moves, a little more depth. So, we're going to add some elements to deepen the story.

> **ACT 1**
>
> Life
>
> Inciting Incident
>
> > **The Big Debate**
>
> Noble Quest
>
> **ACT 2**
>
> > **Meet the Girl** (Subplot Story begins)
>
> Disappointment 1, Y in the Road
>
> Disappointment 2, Y in the Road
>
> **ACT 3**
>
> Disappointment 3
>
> > **Taste of Death**
>
> Help! – Point of No return

Overhaul/Epiphany

Storm the Castle

Perfect Ending!

Let's take a closer look:

ACT 1

Life

Inciting Incident

The Big Debate

Noble Quest

So, your hero is going along with his life, taking the cow to market, and suddenly . . . something happens. You now recognize Life and the Inciting Incident. But now we're going to throw in The Big Debate. See, he's been given an invitation to change his life, to go on a journey of change, to discover new strengths in himself . . . to save the world. Will he take it? The Great Debate is all about your character standing at a crossroads and looking both ways. Which way should he choose? Forward, into Peril, or back, to Safe World? Both choices need to have sufficient motivation. Both need to offer sufficient risk. Eventually, it'll be the hero's overriding PURPOSE that will propel him forward into his Noble Quest, but make sure you build in a sufficient debate before you move him forward.

ACT 2

Meet the Girl (Subplot Story begins)

Disappointment 1

Y in the Road

Whether you're writing a romance or not, you still need to have a hint of romance in your books. Whether it's a traditional romance, or simply the "romance of a friendship"— between women, buddies (many war movies use this device), a father and son, a mother and daughter— every story is deepened by a "romance" subplot. Often, it's in this subplot that your hero will learn the themes of the main plot: forgiveness, trust, hope—whatever you've chosen for your theme. This "love" relationship gives your hero someone else to interact with on the journey, to bounce ideas off of, and eventually learn from. Introduce your Subplot romance shortly after embarking on the Noble Quest, and you'll have a deeper story.

ACT 3

Disappointment 3

Taste of Death

Help! – Point of No Return

So, your character makes the final bad decision, and suddenly all is lost. His fortunes have been reversed, his worst fears are on the horizon. Now, make him lose something close to their hearts. His job, his home, his dog, his best friend. You don't have to actually *kill* someone (although that's a strong device!), but at least kill that something figuratively. You want to bring your character to their lowest point so you can get them on their knees, asking for help. Give them a Taste of Death.

Overhaul/Epiphany

Storm the Castle

Perfect Ending!

Before we can have the Perfect Ending, we need to Storm the Castle. The grand finale. The clash of swords as the bad guy gets his. After your character figures out the Lie he's believed, and discovers the Truth that will set him free, he needs to apply that Truth in battle. We need to see him pick himself up, refortify, see the risks, and summon the courage to Storm the Castle. Maybe he'll rescue the girl. Maybe he'll dispatch the enemy (in increasing order of importance, please. Don't kill off the king before you kill the laughing henchman, unless of course the laughing henchman is the *real* chief villain!). Maybe he'll set the people free. But give us the satisfaction of that final *Huzzah*!

A final note:

Now, remember, your character will need to have sufficient motivation to move forward with each of these new steps. Don't forget to tell us *why* he makes the choices he does!

So now you've discovered the basic structure of your story. Let's put the framework together and then move on to creating the scenes that will fill in the empty spaces and give you your novel!

Your Turn

ACT 1
Life

Inciting Incident

    The Big Debate

Noble Quest

ACT 2
    Meet the Girl (Subplot Story begins)

Disappointment 1

Y in the Road

Disappointment 2

Y in the Road

ACT 3

Disappointment 3

    Taste of Death

Help! – Point of No Return

Overhaul/Epiphany

    Storm the Castle

Perfect Ending!

Step Two: Create

Oh, this is the fun part! All those hours wandering around your house, or locked in your office talking to yourself, consuming countless cups of coffee and eating chocolate chips (okay, so maybe that's only me) are going to pay off. You're going to sit down and write this book. Bring life to your characters.. Finesse your plot. See the magic happen on the page.

Really. I promise.

But here is where you again raise your *write* hand and say: "I am a writer. And I promise not to quit until I've written 'The End.'"
Ready now? Okay, then here's my . . .

Therapist Challenge:

How to write a book in three months, in three hours a day!
(using my organization and book development secrets!)

Write a book in three months? In three hours a day? And have a family lifetoo? Bah!

You laugh, but it can be done. Now, I'm not saying it's easy. But the fact is, with a little "nose to the grindstone," as my father used to say, it's possible.

Here's how:

> If you've read the four keys to a successful writer's life, made the Writer's Pledge, committed to the task, found your writing space, wheedled out time from your schedule, and determined to keep a running game plan, talked to your characters, figured out how to torture them, redeem them and let them live happily ever after, then it's time to talk strategy. How are you going to get those words on the page?

> Let's assume you have twelve weeks to write a thirty chapter book, with approximately 3000 words per chapter. That's 1500 words per scene. That's six pages per writing session, 180 minutes per scene. That's thirty minutes a page.

> Calm down. *Breathe*. Think about it. Can you sit down and write a blog in thirty minutes? What if you already had the idea, already had the words brewing inside you? Probably most of you can. Maybe you can even do it faster than that, but we want to leave room for editing, and revisions, and notes.

> Now, you're going to pad both ends of your three months with two weeks of character development, and two weeks for rewriting and editing, synopsis and a query letter. So, yes, we're talking four months, but really, the concentrated, "under the thought blanket" time (as my kids call it) is three months.

> **Pre-Week 1:** Research of idea and Premise, preliminary characterization, and rough brainstorming of plot. You've already done this!

Pre-Week 2: Further research, the cementing of characterization and Premise writing. Sometimes, a chapter–by–chapter summary of the book helps at this time. We'll be talking about this in the "Publish" section.

Note: There are people who take months in prewriting, and I don't count that as actual novel writing time. They live with their characters in their minds for a while, having conversations, trying on names and attire until they have them just so, and then they embark. During this time, do enough research to get your story plausible and outline the major plot twists in the story. I always write a synopsis at this point, as a guideline.

Then I write my first chapter.

Week 1: Starting day. First, gather your research material around you. Use lots of those big, brightly-colored paper clips so you can bookmark pages. Have a notebook handy. Open up a new file and call it something terrific like "Susie's Super Suspense Book One." Okay, you don't *have* to use my name, butI suppose if you want to . . . . Then, open up a new doc and title it: Chapter 1.

At this point, you're going to turn off your nasty internal editor, the one that tells you things are not grammatically correct, or that you're using a word no one has heard of before. *You're just going to write.* Splash the words onto the page. Ignore the red and green squiggles. *Just write.* A cup of hot cocoa helps, and I'm a big fan of mood music. If you get to a point where you need to do more research, put in something plausible, and denote it with an asterisk (*), which is shorthand for*I'll get back to it.* Don't disrupt your writing flow. If you have a word you hate, yet can't find the right one, asterisk it! If you can't remember a character's name or eye color, asterisk it! When you're done with your manuscript, you'll read through each chapter, do a search for the asterisks, and change them when you're mind isn't cluttered with story.

> ➤ *But what if I come up with a great story thread half way through the scene? Should I stop and go back and fix it?*

NO! Did you hear me? NO! Make a what? *Asterick*! Start writing the story from this point on with your new story thread. Make a note in your notebook to go back and add in or tweak that story thread *after* you've finished the book. Seriously. It's your story. No one will read it until it's done.

Right now you want to is just keep writing, just keep writing . . . .

Once you've finished your scene, *Save*. And then open a new Word document, label it CHAPTER 2 (or maybe Chapter 1, scene 2), and make a few notes about how you'd like to open this scene, or what you want to accomplish. The strategy is to jumpstart your mind the next time you sit down.

Then close the computer. Stand up. Stretch. Dance through the house shouting, "I finished Chapter 1! I finished Chapter 1!" Go to bed, and pray for words for Chapter 2.

If you want, you can spend the weekends doing more research, or going back and rereading any points you wanted to refine.

Weeks 2-12: Keep doing this for the next twelve weeks. You'll be surprised at how disciplined you get, and how fast the words flow out. How empowering it feels to say, "I'll get back to all those asterisks later!"

When you write the final chapter, take a weekend break. Take your poor family out for dinner, for Pete's sake! You'll spend the next two weeks adding in those astounding story threads, re-writing, fixing all the green and red squiggles, and doing a rough edit, then a thorough edit, and then a polish. Okay, it might take you longer than two weeks. But your story is *done*. It's out of your brain. And you can say, ... "Hey! I wrote a book in three months!

Don't panic. I don't expect you to go through *Inside . . . Out and* write your own in twelve weeks. I'm just showing you *how* it could happen.

Take it at your own pace. But look up occasionally. See that light? It's the end of the tunnel.

Here's a hint:

Often your first chapter isn't one you will really use. It is the "finding your character's voice" chapter and really, it contains WAY too much back story to use in the book. But it is helpful as a warm up to the big event.

Let's Make a SCENE!

Okay, so we have created our hero and have some framework to put him into a story. As you begin to interact with your character, it will become clearer how to plug him into the story. I want you to know that writers spend a lot of time on the big picture. So much of writing is the thinking stage.

But eventually, you need to sit down and write the scene. Every book should be made up of a collection of SCENES. Live action we can observe, like a movie. In fact, for me, writing is not unlike viewing a movie. I close my eyes, see the scene, and walk through it with the reader.

How do we create scenes?

Two Types of Scenes

There are two types of scenes, according to Dwight Swain, in the *Techniques of the Selling Writer*.

1. Scenes –contain story action
2. Sequels –contain story response

I'm going to give you a brief overview, then we'll get into the nitty-gritty of the flow and structure of each type of scene. As I've taught these concepts I've discovered a great deal of confusion between the two concepts, mostly because of the word "scene."

So, I've taken the wild liberty of renaming them: **Action** scene and **ReAction** scene.

The Action Scene is the strength of your book. It's the onstage activity.

An Action Scene contains: Goal. Conflict. Disaster.

1. *Goal* – We talked about our character's big-picture goals for the book, aka his PURPOSE. But inside those goals are smaller goals, which are goals derived by the situation, or the character's motivation, or the events happening around him. For every Action Scene, the POV character will have a goal, as will the other characters. The goal must be specific and clearly definable, and it must be a proactive goal, something that makes our character alive and interesting. A character who wants something desperately is an interesting character—someone we want to know or emulate. And this goal helps a reader bond with the character.

2. *Conflict* – These are the obstacles your POV character faces on the way to reaching his goal. You must have conflict in order to make the scene interesting, and to help your character grow. A scene without conflict is a *boring* scene. The conflict can be internal, (competing values), or external, either in interpersonal relationships, or against an external force. But it should be something visible to the reader, and equal in strength to the character's motivation for completing the goal. A conflict that is

too easily overcome isn't a real conflict. That's why bad guys are stronger than good guys—because if they weren't there wouldn't be a story. That's why there is *always* kryptonite in a Superman story. Your story must have conflict.

3. *Disaster* – Don't let your character reach his goal. Winning is boring, except at the end. If a scene ends with victory, then there is no reason to turn the page. Even if there is a small victory with the goal, this victory must launch a new set of obstacles, even worse than before. So in the end, your character is in a worse place. Don't ever end a scene with all the ends tied up. Leave the reader tense and worried!

   The disaster can be found by asking the following questions:
   a. What is the worst thing, externally, (circumstance or physically) that could happen to my character?
   b. What is my character's worst fear at the moment?
   c. What is the worst information my character can receive right now?
   d. What is the worst trouble my character can get into in this scene? Raise the stakes so that they are further from their overall goals.
   e. Have I set up the danger for the readers before the scene begins? (Unexpected, yet plausible)
   f. Have I made my reader *care* about my character? Can they sympathize? (Spell out the stakes often enough so the reader worries!)

To sum up, an Action Scene is an active event where there is a GOAL, a CONFLICT, and a DISASTER. Ideally, at the end of the Action scene, your character should be faced with a choice of some kind, some dilemma they have to solve.

A **ReAction** scene happens after an Action Scene. It can be short, and might be the beginning of another Action Scene, or a separate ReAction Scene. A ReAction Scene uses the information and events of the previous Action Scene and has three components: Response, Dilemma, Decision.

1. *Response* – The emotional and physical follow through to a disaster. You need to give your readers time to deal with the ramifications of what has just occurred in the scene. Your character must process their current state. Often it helps if they can also reiterate the stakes and what their motivations are. Make your character then take stock of his situation, and look at his . . .

2. *Dilemma* – This is the place where there are no good options, and gives the reader and the character the chance to worry and think through the what-ifs. First, they take a look at their options, and state their DILEMMA. Then, they'll look at their choices. Should our hero pursue the prize, or return to the life he knows? Should Frodo give up the ring to the able-bodied Elves, or carry it himself to Mt. Doom? Stating the Dilemma and the choices, as well as the motivations for each, helps the reader get inside the mind of the main character and carry the burdens with him. Eventually, the character will come up with the least-horrible choice, in his opinion. Which leads him to a . . .

3. *Decision* -- The act of making a choice between several options. Your character must have sufficient motivation for his Decision, and of course, it must contain some risk. But if he should succeed, there must also be adequate rewards. He establishes a new

goal, one based on his values and his motivations, and most of all, his Noble Cause. It's important that your character make the Decision for himself. We don't like wishy-washy characters. But make the Decision something that makes sense to the reader, one they can agree with, or at least respect. And make it risky, but something that *might* work. Then your reader will be invested and turn the page. Once the decision is made, then he moves forward.

And now, you're back to an Action Scene, which is why it's such a powerful tool in creating a page turner. A fast-paced story will have ReAction Scenes cut down to the bone. A longer story will draw them out. But they do need to be there, or the reader will forget *why* they're on the journey at all.

For each character, for each story thread, there should be interlacing Action and ReAction Scenes. Some clients have asked me: Does every Action Scene have to be immediately followed by a Reaction Scene? Not necessarily, if the Action Scenes are fast, and tumbling over each other. But at some point, the reader and hero must stop and gather their horses, count their ammo, and figure out what to do next.

A Note about Point of View.

Point of View (POV) is the perspective or viewpoint of your narrating character. The trend now is to have *one* point of view per Action/ReAction scene (not necessarily per chapter). You can separate them out by leaving line breaks or asterisks between the scenes.

For example, Chapter One might look like this:

Action Scene 1 – Your Hero in his Inciting Incident, written from his POV.

Action Scene 2 – Your Heroine, in her Inciting Incident, written from her POV.

Reaction Scene 1 – Your Hero, responding to Action Scene 1 (and possibly Scene 2 if they are together) written from his POV.

Chapter Two might open with: A shortReAction Scene that segues into an Action Scene from the Heroine's POV.

I know you're saying, "What? Wait!" A ReAction and then Action . . . POV . . . I'm so confused. Stay with me here .I know this is confusing, so I'm going to help. I gave you all that information above so you know *what* you're doing. We'll cover POV in more detail later on. But, fleshing it out is really simple, I promise.

Here's how the streamlined Action/ReAction works:

As you enter the scene, regardless of the kind of scene (Action or ReAction), you need to set it up so the reader can keep up with what is in your head:

1. Start with **Setting** (we'll get to that in the next section) and the **Current State of Affairs** (Response and Dilemma).

2.   Then establish the **Goals** (or Decision) of the scene. What does your character hope to accomplish? Of course, sometimes the character doesn't even know,but you, as the author, do know, and you want to hint at the goal.

For example, a woman comes home from her husband's funeral. At the beginning of the scene, as the author, you might say something like:
"Of course, he'd left her with nothing but a giant mortgage, a three-year-old, and a fixer-up list that could wallpaper her cold bedroom." Her goal might be to just go upstairs and climb into bed, and maybe never emerge. She doesn't know that the purpose of the scene is to find his secret will that's hidden under the mattress. No, her goal is to just to go upstairs and deal with her emotions. And then she gets so upset she rips all the sheets off the bed—revealing the envelope containing the will. If you establish these goals at the beginning of the scene, it sets up the elements you can use to cause conflict and create the disaster-ending scene.

3.   Don't forget to fortify the **Motivations** of your character's action and decisions. A woman who has a houseful of guests after a funeral probably isn't going to go to bed. *But*, after her mother-in-law says something terribly harsh (and especially if they have a bad relationship), she might go *hide* in her room. And have a bit of an emotional breakdown. Establish the motivations for every action/decision. That's the end of the ReAction portion of your scene.
4.   Then you move into the Action portion of the scene. You'll have conflict, played out in dialogue and action, and you'll end with a new disaster.

Here's a quick example from my thriller *Wiser than Serpents*, where undercover agent Yanna is hunting for her kidnapped sister, and David, undercover Delta force operative/man who loves her, who didn't know she was mixed up in this until this very moment, escape from Kwan, Yanna's captor.

[Start scene]

[Setting, and Current State of Affairs, goals e.g. the ReAction drawn from the previous scene.]

Think, Yanna, think! Yanna stared up at David, at the horror on his face as he clutched her stupid little knife, and her brain went blank. Aside from being exactly the last scenario she would have conjured up for meeting David again, she knew beyond a shadow of a doubt that right now his brain was checking out every possible egress route from the tiny boat cabin, every possible angle where he wouldn't have to blow his cover to save her life.
    And probably coming up empty.

[Motivation for decision/action]

    Contrary to current appearances, Yanna made her living using her brain and solving problems. And from her viewpoint, David had only one option.

    Kill her, or be killed.

    And, neither of those seemed acceptable. At least, not to her.

[Starting the Action!]

Yanna caught eyes with David. And then, with everything inside her, she kicked out at Kwan's gun hand.[1]

[End scene]

We'll return to this passage later, as we build the other elements of a scene, but hopefully you get the rhythm. It contains a short ReAction, because the book is a fast-paced thriller.

"But I don't write thrillers!"

No problem. **Here's a non-thriller scene, with a longer beginning ReAction.**

This excerpt is from *Finding Stefanie*. Gideon is a subplot character who wakes up in Stefanie's house after a horrible event. He's eighteen and on the run with his two kid sisters.

[Start scene]

[Setting and Hook]

He'd died and gone to paradise. Only, Gideon knew he didn't deserve paradise, so perhaps this was simply a dream. Or maybe just an old west movie, because everything about this place screamed cowboys and horses and an episode of one of those ancient *Lone Ranger* shows. From the warm, dry single bed, with the wool red and black checkered blanket, to the bull riding posters on the walls, the trophies lining the dresser, a coiled rope hung on the bedpost of the other single bed, to more trophies on the opposite dresser. Whoever had lived here had "overachiever" written all over them. Still, Gideon lay in the bed, rested for the first time in – he did the mental math and couldn't remember the last time he hadn't slept with one eye open, waiting for the nightmares, both real and imagined.

[State of Current Affairs, Response]

No nightmares last night. Except, of course, the big one – the fact that he'd burned down the house of mega-rich, mega-star Lincoln Cash. Yes, that should make the news and send the cops running in his direction. Apparently, he still had the knack for knowing how to really blow it, and big. Gideon's eyes had nearly fallen from his sockets when he'd seen the movie star walk up – in fact, he would have considered brain-altering smoke inhalation before he believed that Lincoln Cash owned the house he'd commandeered, and by accessory, incinerated. But Stefanie Noble – she introduced herself and her big brother Nick, the guy who had probably saved his life, when they reached their ranch – had no problem identifying the actor.

[Motivation]

---

[1] [Text Copyright © 2008 by Susan May Warren, Permission to reproduce text granted by Harlequin Books S.A.]

www.learnhowtowriteanovel.com

He wasn't sure what he'd done to deserve Stefanie Noble's loaded shotgun defense – he'd expected to be led off in handcuffs, right back to juvie hall. He made a mental note never to cross Stefanie Noble.

Although it felt good, way too good, to have someone on his side.

[Goals, Decision – Gideon wants to make sure everyone is okay, and then keep moving with his sisters. The last thing he wants is to get caught and have them go back to foster care.]

Especially when she offered him a place to stay, as much as he hated to say yes. But Haley and Macy needed some place warm. One night, he'd told himself. One safe, quiet night. And tomorrow he'd hike back to the ranch, fetch the Impala, pile his sisters inside, and head...somewhere.

(Note: I deleted a bit of backstory here that also described motivation.)
[Okay, now we're moving into the Action scene.]

He sat up, hung his head in his hands. Laughter – was that Haley? -- drifted from the kitchen.

He stood, grabbed his jeans, and shucked them on. Then he crept toward the door. The aroma of breakfast – eggs and sausage? roped him in, and he grabbed his shirt and edged out, into the hall.

[end scene]

Or, you could write an entire 1200-1500 word passage that is *just* a ReAction. It's all about the rhythm of the novel. Just make sure you have the right flow to keep the reader hooked and moving with you through the book.

See—it's not so hard to make a scene, right?

Your Turn:

Chapter 1
POV:
Action Objectives:

Goal:

Conflict:

Disaster:

How will you then start the next (same POV) passage?

Setting:

ReAction:

Dilemma:

Decision:

So where are you going to set your book and your scene?

Setting versus Storyworld!

Setting is a powerful tool in storytelling. It evokes emotion and can be used as another character in the story. The overall setting is essential. it is the setting historical London during WWII? Is it a Kansas farm? Is it Montana? The setting will evoke emotions that draw in your reader. But a great book has more than setting. It also has *Storyworld*!

Storyworld starts, however, with setting, so let's talk about that first.

How do you discover your setting?

1. **Research:** When you're deciding where your story takes place, invest in researching that place. That's why it's good to start with a place you know, because while you're learning all these other techniques, it'll be easier to invest yourself in a familiar setting. But if you don't know it, learn it. Visit the setting. I can't stress this enough. Take pictures, talk to the people, watch people and their mannerisms that are particular to that place.

2. **Observe:** While you're researching, watch for the details that will make a story come to life. Sights, smells, interesting places for scenes to take place. I've had scenes in caves, the Moscow subway, the woods, small airplanes, a monastery, coffee shops, orphanages—even the mall in Washington DC. And I've been fortunate to have gone to all those places. But I've never been in a house on fire—and I had two scenes in *The Perfect Match* inside a burning house. So I talked to firefighters and read as much as I could from personal accounts. And, according to the firefighters I talked to, I got it right. So, it *is* possible to write a scene if you haven't been to the location, if you've done the right research.

   Use people as props. Look around you. Who could be in that scene w``ith your character? People are everywhere, and they can help make a scene unforgettable.

This excerpt is from my journal, something I wrote while waiting for a train on the pier in Vladivostok:

Pigeons waddle in the center of the square, over grey cobblestones, searching for treasures, their heads bobbing like royalty.

A couple wrapped in a love pretzel . . .

A sullen man with distant eyes, one of them so mangled from a recent run-in with a fist, it glowed red-blood. He gazed out over the harbor, flicking suspicious glances in my direction.

Across the square, two long-gone drunks search the ads in the paper as if reading the stock quotes. Two benches down, a couple women, their pudgy bodies squeezed into black leggings and fluorescent pink tee-shirts prop each other up, feigning sleep.

The smells of diesel fuel, fresh fish, and dust laden the humid breeze.

The sound of a welder grinds (hisses, snarls...I was searching for the right word) in the background amid the clank and whistles of a working shipyard.

In the far distance, the mangled voice of the train loudspeaker drones announcements.

Overhead, the sky is an enigmatic, mysterious gray, neither ominous nor hopeful, shedding (or casting) a dismal (or despondent) theme upon us travelers.

Obviously, I'm a people watcher, But if you can't go to your setting, watch movies filmed there, get maps and travel books, read about the area via non-fiction or fiction books. Ask people who've been there about their impressions, or search the Internet for information. Consider consulting a Chamber of Commerce site.

3. **Mood:** When you're choosing your setting for your scene, find a place that will work to create conflict for the POV character, whether it's the mood the scene evokes, or whether it provides physical opposition to your character's goals. For example, in one scene in *The Perfect* Match, my character had to investigate a burned out building.. Her goal? To prove herself capable and independent so she could get the job of Fire Chief. However, the setting itself provided the conflict, because it was dangerous, and she found herself in a predicament that devastated her goals.

What is Storyworld?

Storyworld is the sounds, smells, tastes, touch, and rich, focused visual details that convey the impressions, opinions, and overall state of emotion of the POV character, and in turn, the reader.

Storyworld is more than setting, however. You need to know and understand your setting, but that's just one aspect of Storyworld. I want you to start thinking of your Storyworld as the third character in your novel. Middle Earth. WW II London. Mitford. Narnia. Oz. Wherever your story is set, it will have a character, a feeling to it that lends itself to the story, and works either with your characters, or against them.

A book without a Storyworld is like watching a movie without the setting, a play without props. Sure we'll use our imaginations, but we have to work harder to do it. Set up your Storyworld correctly and your reader moves freely about the book.

Creating Storyworld

Building a Storyworld is simply about gathering up your elements, and then putting them together, using a few tricks.

    ✓ **Just the facts, ma'am.**

Let's start with the basics: the Five Ws. Who, What, Where, When, Why. The reader needs to know *who* is in the scene, *what* is going on around them, *where* it is, *when* it is, , and a little about *why* they are there.

I'll use my book *Nothing But Trouble* (Tyndale, May 2009) to show you how I built t Storyworld.

Let's start by making a chart:

> Who – PJ Sugar, bad girl turned good
>
> Where – back in her home town, at her parents' country club
>
> When – Memorial Day weekend
>
> What – PJ's driving up and wrestling the courage to go inside, other cars are also driving up and people are carrying presents
>
> Why – for her sister's wedding

But we're just getting started. Once we've figured out each of these elements, we need to go deeper:

Who – What is the state of mind of the POV character walking into the scene? In one or two words, define how the POV character feels.

Where – What details stands out to the character? Why is this significant to the character?

When is it – What is the time of year, and how do we know that? We're looking for details here.

What – What other activities are going on in the scene? What is your POV character doing?

Why – Why is she/he in this place?

Going back to our chart:

Who: PJ Sugar – feeling like a duck out of water, especially after being in a car for two days, but also because she's been out of the high-society lifestyle her parents raised her in. She's tense and grimy and uncomfortable and just wants to run.

Where: She's back in a place where she got into trouble. She notices the new addition to the kitchen (we'll find out why later) and the changes made to the country club in her absence, as well as the similarities—the pool, for example. It's a place of rich, albeit difficult, memories for her.

When: June—so the lilacs are blooming, the flowers are out in pots on the verandah, the sprinklers are spraying the golf course.

What: A Mercedes pulls up and a well-groomed guest gets out holding a beautifully wrapped gift (of course PJ doesn't have one). Also, she's driving a Bug, and in the parking lot are Beemers, Mercedes, and Lexus's. PJ is brushing potato chip crumbs off her lap.

Why: She's here because her sister *begged* her to come and watch her son while she goes on her honeymoon. PJ returns because she longs to start over again.

So, now we have PJ's state of mind and some of the details of the scene. But we're not ready to build yet.

✓ **Observations – What's in your world?**

To really draw yourStoryworld, you need to use your five senses to engage the reader's emotions. Sight. Smell. Sound. Touch.Taste. When you walk into a room, all your senses are a part of your understanding of that scene.

Smell is a huge memory tool, and, just like you, your character will remember them.

Sound is essential. Rarely is there a place without some noise in it, yet we often don't read about it or hear it in a scene. Imagine watching a movie without the sound.

Sight, of course, is what a scene is usually built on, but remember those specific, mood-enhancing details.

Touch is also important. Your character can rub her hand on the soft, worn leather of a desk chair or dig her fingers into the rough bark of an oak tree.

Taste is active in our memory too. We taste things in our memory.Your heroine could taste her fear. She tasted her past, the memory of sitting in the kitchen with her mother, sneaking cookie dough out of the bowl.

Before you sit down to write, make a sensory list of everything you perceive in that scene. You'll use it as a "cheat sheet" as you build the scene.

Let's take a look at how to build the five senses into a scene:

This scene is from *Taming Rafe*, set in New York City in the summer:

Sitting in his pickup, staring at himself—all twenty feet of glowing hot neon in the center of Times Square—Rafe Noble realized what a fake he'd become. The image shone for thirty seconds, then flipped to an advertisement of *America, Now!* magazine, on which Rafe's face graced this month's cover.

They'd airbrushed the growl right off of him, made him look downright tame. (His feelings about being there.)

The light changed, and he surged forward into traffic on Forty-Second Street. Heat slithered into the cab of his 1984 Ford pickup, the air conditioner barely able to stay ahead of the furnace outside. (TOUCH) It was the heat wave of the century in New York City, and he'd agreed to appear at some hoity-toity charity event.

How he hated this town and the smells of grilling lamb from the gyro stands, the cigarette smoke, the trash fermenting in the piles of black bags on the sidewalk, the bus exhaust fouling the air. (SMELLS) He hated the sounds of brakes squealing, the cabbies arguing for space, the cheeps of pigeons fighting for crumbs. (SOUNDS) The few times he'd been here, he'd cut his trips short, needing open spaces like the rest of the city needed air-conditioning.

The place had nearly choked him with the press of people packing the sidewalks, and he'd practically fled the city, gulping in the open space of his Texas ranch like a drowning man.

(TASTE)

He cut a left at the next light, then slammed on his brakes before he plowed over a couple of fast-walking suits arguing into their Blackberries. (SIGHT, BUT ALSO A SOUND)

Using the five senses helps the story come alive, and puts the reader right into the scene.

Let's go back to PJ sitting in her car, brushing potato chip crumbs from her lap.

Build the five senses:

Sound: Birds singing. Kids splashing in the pool. The hiss of sprinklers.

Smell: Freshly cut grass from the golf course, the smell of the club restaurant—maybe steaks grilling on the deck. Chlorine from the pool. Hot vinyl seats? The baking pavement?

Touch: She feels grimy, so maybe her legs stick to the vinyl seat, or crumbs have gone down her shirt? Maybe the tingle of greasy hair, or the feel of cotton across her teeth? Maybe there's a wind blowing and it curls into her car.

Taste: This can be a memory of actually tasting something, the sweet tang of ice cream on her tongue. Or it can be a feeling. She could taste the dread, welling like acid in the back of her throat.

Sight: The lilacs hanging from the trees, the pots overflowing with thick impatiens on the porch, the aqua blue of the pool.

All you're doing is creating a thesaurus, a pool of images to pull from as you're creating your scene/Storyworld.

But we're still not done!

✓ **Voices . . . or "How do ya like yer yellers?"**

Building Storyworld isn't just about putting your character into the world. It's also about moving your character through it. A static Storyworld is boring. We need to see your character engage with his surroundings. And that means they need to interact. Which means dialogue.

I used to live in Tennessee. And I'll never forget the first time I walked into *The Southern*, a restaurant with foreign food like grits and chicken-fried steak, a name which still confuses me. I'll never forget the waitress, a woman in a pink and white uniform, smacking down an egg-stained menu in front of me. When I ordered eggs and bacon, she aske, "How do ya like yer yellers?"

Your world has people in it and they talk. How *do* they talk? What colloquialisms do they use? How do they say different things?

Consider this scene from *Taming Rafe*:

> They pulled up to the unpainted house. It sat in a dip between two weather-beaten, grassless hills. The effects of the last dust storm had piled dirt against the barn and porch. Dirty curtains flapped from the open windows, and a pot of dead geraniums told her that Mrs. Thatcher—God rest her soul—had been a woman of hope.
>
> Matthias's bulk jiggled the car as he got out. "Preacher's inside. Hurry up."
>
> Mary thought he might grab her case from the jump seat, but he marched into the house without so much as a glance backward.
>
> She had no time for tears. Rosie needed a home. She needed work. Mary eased open the door. Weakness rushed through her, a ripple of despair that had the ability to crumple her. She couldn't do this. A tear squeezed out, and she wiped it against Rosie's head, brushing her lips against her daughter's skin.
>
> "Mary!" Thatcher stood on the porch, the preacher behind him.
>
> She saw anger in his eyes and stiffened. *Please, Lord, help me.*
>
> "Can I get your case for you, ma'am?" The voice beside her, a soft drawl, seemed calm against her racing heart.

I hope you can hear the difference between the hero and the villain. But also, you can guess the time period by the dialogue. Matthias says, "Preacher," an old- fashioned term for the pastor. Instead of "bag" or "suitcase" a character says "case," a term used in the early 1900s, or even before. And then, "ma'am." Up in Yankee country, the only people who use "ma'am" are servicemen and cops who pull you over. Down in the south, however, it's much more common.

Figure out what speech or dialect is particular to your setting, and insert it into your scene.

 If you don't have dialogue in your scene, one way is to throw in signs, like I did with Rafe and the neon blinking Times Square sign. But a weathered sign tacked up to an old oak pointing the way to "Ender's Holler" would also speak volumes about your Storyworld.

So, let's go back to our scene we're building for PJ and apply the Voices.

We're in Minnesota. We Minnesotans are non-conflict people. We say things like, "Whatever" and "You betcha" and "That's quite a deal." We're not really expressing opinions, it's more like a placeholder, an acknowledgement that two people are in the same room. So, if I were to write PJ's scene, I might throw in a "whatever" or a "you betcha."

Or even show the sign to the country club, and how it's elegant and snooty.

Now, this is where we start really sharpening our writing.

We've already gathered our anchoring elements—the Five Ws, and filled out the five senses. We've also thrown in some dialect or speech elements. ***Now we want some details that really make the scene specific and create the emotional connection with the reader.***

✓ **Emotions: The devil is in the details**

Think: What is the *one* detail you could highlight that captures this Storyworld in a nutshell?

New York – a cabbie, gesturing out the window, his dark eyes saying more than his sign language. It communicates the "don't get in my way" feeling of Manhattan.

Montana – a pair of cowboys, nursing cups of coffee in the middle of a sunny afternoon, their boot heels hooked onto the low rungs of the barstools. Doesn't that convey the "slow down and don't worry" sanguine aura of the west?

Moscow – the precise placement of the red brick cobblestones, nearly three football fields long, shadowed by the hovering expanse of the Kremlin over Red Square. Doesn't that juxtapose the life of the communist worker and the control of the government?

What you're looking for in the scene is a metaphorical statement that conveys the sense *of the place. The* emotion *you want to convey in the scene.*

Look at your scene: What metaphors do you see embedded in the scene? Think of it as a pool of objects, from which you'll pluck one to create the feeling you'd like to convey.

Let's think about Florida. The ocean, a common metaphor for new beginnings, or fears. Waves, washing away something, or bringing in something new. Or what about Colorado? Mountain peaks—challenge and adventure. New York—crowded, choking. or opportunity and hope?

What are you trying to convey, and is that metaphor already in your scene?

PJ wants to fit into her former world, but doesn't know how. She's no longer used to the country club life, but she can easily remember fitting into it. I use the sight of the new addition to the building to show that maybe some things, once destroyed, can never fit in again.

We're almost ready. And you may have already done this in your five senses and metaphor search, but now I'm going to let you in on a secret.

Use *Specific* Language. Specific nouns and details do more to evoke emotions and create place than commonalities. Rhododendron is different than Bougainvillea. And they grow in different places. As do birch trees and cottonwoods. And they also look different. A mahogany desk is different than a metal office desk, and arouses different emotions. I could have said the smells of New York nauseated Rafe. Instead I described them, using specific details.

Do this with every Storyworld. You won't use all of your notes, but make a list of items particular to each Storyworld. This is especially important when working with historical novels. Clothing, cars, architecture. Do your research and know the world you're entering.

Let's put our Storyworld together

The five Ws, the five senses, the dialogue or speech, the metaphor and the details.; Think of a movie scene, starting wide and then zooming in closer, adding texture as we go.

The Scene: PJ's in her car, driving along Main Street.

She (PJ) had the urge to toe off her flip-flops and drive barefoot as she turned off Main at the theater, driving past the red-bricked high school, then out to the country club, with its neat hedges, its white terraces, the tidy golf course. Before she could stop herself, her gaze swept the employee parking lot for his Kawasaki. (Start wide, pull in close, add dialogue.)

"You'll be back someday. And maybe I won't be here." Boone's voice, low and angry.

Oh, she dearly hoped so.

The new kitchen wing, now nearly ten years old, jutted out past the old foundation. It felt too much like visiting a war monument. She had the urge to stand over it, say a little prayer for lives lost.

Namely, hers. (Metaphor)

She pulled up at the far end of the parking lot, cataloguing the changes. The weathered, white-tiled pool boasted a new slide and, on the high dive that had once trapped her at the pinnacle, a fresh coat of paint. A crisp white flag fluttered on the tenth tee, in plain sight to anyone who might be looking.

She hadn't really noticed that before, and for a second, nearly put her car into reverse. But it wasn't likely that she'd see old Ben Murphy or Ernie Hoffman again, was it? Or that they'd still remember finding her entangled with Boone in a sea of mauve chiffon on the smooth putting green blanket.

Behind her, a guest slammed the door to her silver BMW, balancing in her arms a gift wrapped in pink. PJ glanced in the rearview mirror. Why hadn't she stopped outside town to change? No, she had to show up smelling like she'd spent a week under a bridge, her short red—no, auburn—hair greasy, in frayed jeans, a tank and flip-flops.

"Oh, boy..." She sat in the car, hands wrapped around the steering wheel, debate gluing her to the seat. "Oh . . . boy."

"Don't even think about coming back here, PJ Sugar. We'll arrest you on sight." PJ closed her eyes against Director Buckam's warning in her ears. Just because she'd been banned from the country club premises ten years ago didn't mean they'd recognize her today. She was taller, for one. And not wearing chiffon.

Whoever is in Christ is a new creation, the old has gone, the new has come.

Right. The New and Improved PJ Sugar.

Her cute little lime green bug looked pedestrian and forlorn as she grabbed her bag off the front seat, got out of the car, and climbed the broad, white steps, pushing open the door to enter the grand foyer. Polished wood, worked leather, Turkish wool rugs—the smells of tradition rushed back to her. She smelled Sunday lunches on the verandah, Saturday morning swimming lessons, heard the slap of wet feet running through the main hall from the locker rooms, and felt anew the air conditioning prickling her skin before she hit the humidity of the summer. She could almost see Boone in his caddie uniform, his wide shoulders under the green polo shirt grooming him into the preppie boy his father hoped to create. How one could hide behind the aspirations of an ambitious parent.

"Hey baby, want to go down to Hal's after I get off work?"

You get the scene: PJ wants to embrace the memories, but she can't get past the shame, and the sense she doesn't belong.

Ways that I convey that? Aside from the internal monologue, you have words like "prickling" and of course, "War Monument," and "lives lost." Especially the crisp white "surrender" flag from the tenth tee, which we find out later was a pivotal location in her life.

Now for a few tricks:

Don't frontload the Storyworld. The key to building a great Storyworld is weaving this in between the action. The passage above was pulled out and put together from a longer scene, filled with other action, like people getting out of cars. Storyworld should be three to five sentences at the most. Even the last paragraph had only four sentences of Storyworld. Long passages of description tire the reader, but we need to see the world, so weave it in.

Think *action*. Give your character something to do in the scene, don't just have him or her stand still, looking around. Maybe he's buying a hotdog from a New York City vendor. Or ordering eggs and bacon at a greasy spoon. Or asking directions. Or trying to find someone or something. As your character moves through the scene, you describe it without the reader even realizing that they're slowly being drawn into the world.

Use nuance to trick your reader. Use verbs that convey the emotion of the scene: prickling, wet feet slapping the floor (running, fleeing), prayer, gluing, hiding. Although the verbs are used in different places, subconsciously they raise the sense of dread for the entire scene.

Use one of the five sense every now and again to draw readers in. Just like interspersing the world between actions, sprinkle the senses throughout the scene, enabling your reader to see or taste or hear the Storyworld. If you don't, it's like the sound suddenly going off in the movie!

Storyworld is the one thing you can do that will make your reader want to revisit your world over and over. Expend the effort to do it right.

Your Turn:

Pick an early scene in your WIP to work on, maybe your Inciting Incident, or a scene just after that. Now, let's build your Storyworld:

Who –

What –

Where –

When –

Why –

Smells –

Sounds – (including voices!)

Sights –

Touch –

Taste –

Details you could use for a metaphor –

Now you have your cheat sheet. Go create your Storyworld!

The Use of Perspective in Storyworld

So, you already know that every book, regardless of what kind—suspense, romance, fantasy, thriller, historical romance—every book starts out someplace. In a world. At a moment. With a person. What we also call "the news."

A good way to see Storyworld is to watch the opening scenes of a movie. Note the details of the scene and how they work with the five senses.

However, without a frame of reference, a perspective through which to view these details, we don't understand the significance of what we're seeing. We need to make our Storyworld *personal*.

My book *Wiser than Serpents* (remember the David and Yanna excerpt?) starts in a night market in Taiwan. I could have started with description: the hundreds of tables pushed side by side, vendors hawking chicken legs and squid on a stick, the cloying smell of sweet potatoes mixed with the pungency of tea eggs. I could have talked about the voices of the vendors, each rising above the other in a wild, chaotic cacophony that outshouted even the seagulls at the nearby shipyards.

However, if I simply *describe* the scene, then the reader doesn't know how to interpret what they see. They need a character to perceive the sights and sift the details through that character's grid of understanding. Scenery without interpretation is, well, *boring*.

Yet, put someone in the scene with a purpose, even something at stake, and it becomes compelling. What if they're looking for a small boy, lost in the crowd? Every vendor would be suspect, every vat of boiling oil a horror. Or, what if your character is hiding from someone? Suddenly the market becomes their salvation. What if they're hungry, and have no money? Then the night market becomes tantalizing, perhaps pushing them over the edge.

Here's the secret: Move your character through the scene, experiencing the *details* as they go, and the scene changes from static to alive.

Storyworld is the News and the Senses filtered through your
POV character's opinions, fears, dreams and goals.

He'd never eaten deep fried frog on a stick, but David Curtiss was a patriot, and he'd do just about anything for his country.

"*Shei Shei*," he said as he took the delicacy from the vendor, fished out a New Taiwan Dollar, and dropped it into the vendor's hand.

He wondered what might leave a worse taste in his mouth, fried frog, or meeting a man who had beheaded the two undercover agents that had tried this trick before David. But if all went as planned, his culinary sacrifice would lead him to the identity of Kwan-Li, leader of the Twin Serpents, the largest organized crime syndicate in eastern Asia.

The smells of night market were enough to turn even his iron gut to mush—body odor, eggs boiled in soy sauce, fresh fish and oil redolent from the nearby shipyard. Even worse, the fare offered in the busy open market sounded like something from a house of horrors menu: Grilled chicken feet, boiled snails, breaded salamander, poached pigeon eggs, and the specialty of the day — carp head soup.

"What did you get me into, Chet?" he whispered, wondering if Chet Stryker, his cohort for his unfortunate op, were grinning at the other end of his transmitter. "Squid, or even snails, okay, but a frog?" Chet had set up this meet—and the frog signal. "Next time, you're going to be drinking asparagus juice, buddy." He hoped Chet's silence meant he still had eyes on him. David hadn't seen his partner in the forty-five minutes he'd been walking around the market—a sign of Chet's skill, no doubt.

David looked at the brown and crispy frog and wondered if he was supposed to add condiments — he'd noticed a sort of ketchup, and horseradish at the bar.

A few more seconds and he'd have to take a bite. It wasn't enough to just stand here and try to blend with the crowd—not an easy task given that every man who brushed by him stood around chin height. Even with David's long black dyed hair, silk Asian shirt and designer jeans he knew he looked like a walking American billboard. Thankfully, foreigners flocked to the novelty of night market in this part of Kaohsiung in Taiwan.

He saw a couple of Americans stroll by, listened to their comments about the food, the smells. A short blonde, slightly pudgy, wearing a blue Taiwanese shirt and shorts set probably purchased in a local beach shop, sucked on the straw of a Ju Ju Bee shake. Next to her, her husband was finishing off a grilled squid. Aid workers, probably—the island had a plethora of Americans working in relief and humanitarian aid agencies. Especially after the last earthquake.

He checked his watch. Kwan's man was late. Which meant he'd have to take a bite of froggie.

He lifted the amphibian to his mouth.[2]

---

[2] Text Copyright © 2008 by Susan May Warren; Permission to reproduce text granted by Harlequin Books S.A.

Everything that happens in night market is through David's eyes, as he's waiting for his contact. Because it's a thriller, I go right into the action, but I still want readers to know where they are.

So what are the tricks to adding your POV character's perspective?

✓   Internal thought that lends itself to opinion.

e.g.   *He wondered what might leave a worse taste in his mouth . . .*

Ask: How does he feel about being there? Positive, negative, uncomfortable, scared? What would he be thinking? Layer those thoughts into the scene.

✓   Senses that add attitude.

e.g. *The smells of night market were enough to turn even his iron gut to mush . . .*

Ask: What physical reaction—and to what?—could he have that would strengthen his opinion or attitude about this situation?

✓   Statements that reveal his mood through opinionated nouns and verbs.

e.g. . . .*Which meant he'd have to take a bite of froggie.*

Can you feel the derision? But, what if I wrote:

e.g. *He couldn't wait to take a bite of the delectable treat.*

Doesn't make sense, not with the rest of the paragraph, does it?

But, what about these folks?

He saw a couple of Americans stroll by, listened to their comments about the food, the smells. A short blonde, slightly pudgy, wearing a blue Taiwanese shirt and shorts set probably purchased in a local beach shop sucked on the straw of a Ju Ju Bee shake. Next to her, her husband was finishing off a grilled squid.

Now, *that* male POV character might say, "It was a delicatessen of exotic treats that made his palate water."

Make the perspective personal!

Your Turn:

How does your POV character feel about being in the Storyworld?

What one internal thought could he have that reveals this feeling?

What physical response does he have that reveals his feeling/attitude? Think: Senses cause physical responses.

What noun, adjective or verb could you use that adds prejudice to his thoughts, speech or actions?

Where and how do you start your book or scene?

Hook 'em!

> "One of the most difficult things is the first paragraph. In the first paragraph, you solve most of the problems with your book. The theme is defined, the style, the tone. At least in my case, the paragraph is a kind of sample of what the rest of the book is going to be."
>
> Gabriel Garcia Márquez, who won the 1982 Nobel Prize for Literature for *One Hundred Years of Solitude,* which sold over 10 million copies

I have Márquez's quote taped to my computer monitor, to remind me of the impact and the importance of that Hook paragraph.

What do you do when you pick up a book? Probably read the back cover blurb, and then open to the first page. Then, in the next ten seconds, you'll either be hooked or you'll put the book down. An author has to capture your interest—and every other potential reader's interest—in the first couple of sentences. A reader is looking for creative writing, a question that piques their interest, someone they can relate to, a setting that interests them, and a story that can match the value of their time. That's a lot to put into the first sentence, or even the first paragraph!

But it can be done, especially if you make your Hook SHARP.

What do I mean by that? A SHARP Hook is a Hook comprised of the five elements that will hook your reader into continuing the story::

Stakes

Hero/Heroine Identification

Anchoring

Run

Problem/Story Question

Stakes – Making them big, scary, and intimate

Why does this story matter? This is the question every reader is going to ask themselves, if not out loud, then silently, as they're reading. Why, indeed, should anyone spend time reading your book?

Stakes drive your reader through the story, and hinting at the stakes in the beginning will give your reader something to fight for.

There are two kinds of stakes: **public** or **private.**

Stakes can be public, meaning they affect society, as in in movies like *Raiders of the Lost Ark, The Hunt for Red October*, or even *Erin Brockovich*), or private, as in some of my favorites movies: *Frequency, Cellular*, or even the poignant *Somersby*). The important element is that if the stakes matter to you, they'll matter to your readers.

Public Stakes

Public stakes have much to do with public values. For example, during WW II, the public value was very much protecting our country, and banding together to fight the war. So, stories about espionage and battle were popular stakes in both books and movies.

However, as times have changed, so have our values.

Today, personal freedom and family have taken over as the chief collective stakes. We still have issues of national security, which is why shows like *24* are so popular). But even within those issues, it's the *personal life* behind the war that captures people. Think of shows like *Army Wives*. When stakes involve our freedoms and safety as Americans, or members of a family, it makes for a compelling story.

One example is the movie *Saving Private Ryan*. Even the main character, Captain John Miller, played by Tom Hanks, realizes the power of family against the great backdrop of the war as he fights to bring home Private Ryan to his devastated mother.

Ask: Is the issue in the story pertinent to today's public values? Does the issue touch the heart of all of us? Does it tap into the American Dream?
Ask: What matters to me? If something matters to you, then it matters to others. What's the worst thing you could think of happening to you? Others will fear the same thing too. And that's where you find your public stakes.

But what if my story is about a prairie girl who wants to win a horse race? There's no public stakes there.

Who can forget the story of Laura Ingalls, when she rides her horse Bunny in a race against Nellie? Evil Nellie hates that Laura has a horse, and persuades her mother to buy her a fancy horse from Mankato. Laura's horse doesn't have a chance in the race against Nellie's thoroughbred. What's worse, Mrs. Olsen mocks Caroline, Laura's mother, for being poor, and refuses to sell her shoes for her children until she has cash. If Laura can win the race, she'll receive a prize that she can use to pay for the shoes. She trains Bunny and is ready for the big race. Then Willie, Nellie's brother, gets sick. No one is around, so Laura has to make a choice: ride Bunny to fetch the doctor and risk the horse being too tired to run the race, or let Willie suffer. What will she do?

Why does this story matter?

See, underneath this story are two competing values: Family honor and compassion, both of which Laura has big doses of.

> Which value will win? This is what we call **Private Stakes.**

Private stakes can be found in the root of our values. The things that drive us, or the things we long for. Laura longed to show up Nellie, and to help her parents. But she also knew that to be true to herself, she had to be compassionate. When we pit values against each other in a story, it not only makes for great conflict, but it touches the heart of your readers in a way that makes the story stick.

How do you find those private values of your character? Earlier we talked about finding the identity of your character and following that down to his values. Here are some simple questions to help you find those values.

> *Ask*: What matters most to him in life?
>
> *Ask*: What would he avoid at all costs, and why?
>
> *Ask*: What defining incident in his past has molded him to the person he is today?
>
> *Ask*: What are his goals, and why?

Find two different values, and then ask yourself: In what situation will these values be pitted against each other? That situation showcases your private stakes.

Hero/Heroine Identification

How do you create sympathy and connection with your readers?

We're only going to read a book about someone we can, at least remotely, relate to. Someone we can understand. Maybe they don't live in the same culture we do, or they lived 200 years ago, or maybe they're from another planet, but if they care about the same things we care about, or if they find themselves in a situation we might find ourselves in, then we can identify with them. Creating that piece of identification at the start will give our readers enough of a connection to entice them to let our characters into their lives.

I'm going to use an example from my own collection of books: *Flee the Night*.

My heroine is an ex-CIA agent, on the run from a crime she is accused of committing years ago. Not many of us have been accused of a crime and are on the run from an international assassin. However, many of us have had a secret we don't want revealed, and it was this collective sympathy that I used when crafting the first line:

> **The past had picked the worst time to find her.**

I go on in the paragraph to insert another element of sympathy, or identification with the reader. The heroine's daughter is traveling with her, and if my heroine is killed, her daughter is also in jeopardy.

How do find that sympathetic element?

- ✓ Ask yourself: What do I have in common with my character? What need, or dream, or situation, or fear, or past experience do we share?
- ✓ And what facet of that can I extrapolate and fit into my story?

Give your reader a reason to *care* about your character, something that touches his/her own life, and they'll turn the page to see what happens!

Anchoring

How do you pull your readers into the Storyworld?

So many books these days start out with dialogue or action, leaving the reader to guess the *where* and *when* and even to some extent, the *who*. You, on the other hand, want your reader to know where they stand in a book, what the world is like, who the players are, and why they're there. And you want to do it in a way that helps your reader capture the mood and framework of the book. By the end of the first paragraph, and for sure the first scene, you should have anchored your character into the scene by using the Five Ws: Who, What, Where, When, and Why.

Since we touched on this in the previous Storyworld section, I'm just going to give a short example here. Here's a continuation of the previous sample scene from *Flee the Night*.

> The past couldn't have picked a worse time to find her.

> Trapped in seat 15A on an Amtrak Texas Eagle chugging through the Ozarks at 4:00 a.m. on a Sunday morning, Lacey . . . Galloway . . . Montgomery—what was her current last name?—tightened her leg lock around the computer bag at her feet.

We know who our character is, where she is, and what the timeframe is, so we know the Who, the Where, and the When. Lacey has fictitious last names, which raises the element of mystery. We can safely suppose that a person who has an alias might be afraid of something and on the run. This information, along with Lacey guarding her computer bag for some reason, gives us the What. These are four of the Five Ws. The only W missing is the Why.We don't know "why" she's doing the "what."

> She dug her fingers through the cotton knit of her daughter's sweater as she watched the newest passenger to their compartment find his seat. Lanky, with olive skin and dark eyes framed in wire-rimmed glasses, it had to be Syrian assassin Ishmael Shavik who sat down, fidgeted with his leather jacket, then impaled her with a dark glance.

The fifth W (Why) is addressed here. Lacey is afraid because she is on a train with an assassin who recognizes her. Note the words I use to create fear: Trapped. Chugging (can you smell smoke?), lock, dug, impaled. These words give a sense of doom and set the mood of the paragraph.

Well used, the Five Ws can evoke emotions and give us a feeling of happiness, tension, or even doom in the scene.

Try this:

- ✓ What is the one emotion you'd like to establish in this first sentence, paragraph, or scene?
- ✓ Using the Five Ws, what words can you find for each category that conveys this sense of emotion? Use these in the crafting of your first paragraph.

On the Run

Have you started your scene in the middle of the action?

Dwight Swain, in *Techniques of the Selling Writer*, says ". . . a good story begins in the middle, retrieves the past and continues to the end."

A good hook already has your character in the middle of the Inciting Incident, or at least prefaces it with foreshadowing. It's a blip in time in the middle of that incident that zeros in on the character and gives us a glimpse at his life and why this situation is important.

For example, in the previous excerpt, Lacey is on the train, and the assassin has already walked on board when we open the story. If we started it ten minutes earlier, we'd have to wade through the backstory and setting. We would have to start with Lacey relaxing on the train, and then ramp up the tension when the assassin walks in. Although that might work, starting the story two steps into the Inciting Incident heightens the tension, and we are drawn into the scene.

Let's take another story. How about *Reclaiming Nick*?

When the lanky form of Saul Lovell walked into the Watering Hole Café, dragging with him the remnants of the late April chill, Nick Noble knew that his last hope of redemption had died.

This is not a high-action scene, but the lawyer is coming into the café, and we know that Nick had redemption at stake before he walked in. The scene is already unfolding as we join Nick. Notice we also have Who, Where, When, as well as some precise words that convey a sense of dismay: dragging, chill, died.

The paragraph continues with a glimpse at what Nick is up to:

> Nick didn't have time to deal with the arrival of his father's lawyer. Not with one fist wrapped in the collar of Stinky Jim's duster and a forearm pinning his cohort Rusty to the wall.
>
> "We were simply offering to buy her lunch," Rusty snarled.

The first paragraph tells us that Nick has some sort of "protector" element about him (creating sympathy and a touch of heroism). Whether he's a bouncer, or a cop, we don't know. And we know that something has happened to his father, because his father's lawyer shows up.

It's *so* easy to give into the temptation and start at the beginning. We want people to know and love our character, to understand them, to understand *why* this situation so rocks their world.

Trust me, it's much more fun for the reader to figure it out on the run than to front load that information.

One of my favorite shows is *Lost*. The writers totally won me when they opened their first season with a shot of a plane down and people wandering the beach. I didn't have to know their backgrounds to understand that they were shocked and scared, and to feel instantly sorry for them. The fun of the series has been figuring out who they all are, and how they fit together.

Problem

When all is said and done, what is your story about?

This is the last element, and probably the most important element, in creating a hook: the Problem, or identifying the Story Question.

We already talked at length about Story Question in the section "The Four Things All Stories Must Have." Just to recap: The story question is the one thematic question that drives the book. Will Richard Kimball ever find out who killed his wife? Will Frodo be able to destroy the ring? This question permeates the hero's and/or heroine's every decision throughout the story, and needs to be hinted at in the first sentence, in the first paragraph, and in the first scene of your novel.

How do you incorporate all these elements? It can be daunting, I know from personal experience. If you have to, for your own rough draft purposes, write the story from the beginning. Then, about a paragraph after the Inciting Incident, search for your first sentence. It's in there, I promise.

Then, copy and paste this first sentence into a new Word document, and start your first chapter there.

If you don't want to do all that, here's another technique I often use. I stop the action about two to five minutes into my brain and I interview my character. "How are you feeling now? Are you surprised? What is at stake? Give me one sentence to explain your current situation to an onlooker." I take these answers and use them to form that first sentence, as well as the first paragraph.

So, let's look at some of *my* attempts to create a hook. It can take few trys! This is the premise of a book I'm working on called *Where there's Smoke* (a romantic suspense). After I give you the premise and some pertinent information, I'll share a couple of sample hooks with you.

When wildland photographer Kacie Billings moves home to Ember, Montana, all she wants is to earn redemption for her part in the accidental death of five firefighters. But redemption doesn't come easy when she runs right into Hotshot Boss Jed Ransom, the man who saved her life while his crew died. Jed isn't interested in payback—he just wants to forget that day on the mountain and start again. But memories and blame aren't easily extinguished, and it seems as though someone is after Kacie. In a season of forest fires, Jed and Kacie are about to discover that where's there's smoke . . . there's death.

What you need to know: Kacie's father died in a firestorm years ago, and the arsonist was never caught.

Stakes: Public – a repeat of the previous loss: five firefighters killed

Private – (Kacie) – saving firefighters versus finding her father's killer

Heroine Identity: facing what her father faced and knowing that part of him/guilt for her mistakes.

Anchoring: windy, out of control, heat, dirt, a feeling of looming danger

Run: At the point either right when the flames are consuming her, or just before it, as they are running toward her.

Problem: Will she ever escape the grip fire has on her life?

Here are my samples and the elements I included are listed after each hook.

> It was a cool August day, on the south slope of the Klondike ravine, that Kacie Billings caught her first glimpse of hell. She framed it in her viewfinder: a wall of orange clawing toward the group of raccoon-eyed hotshots, all grinning up at her under their grimy red helmets, in their flag-yellow Nomex shirts, as if they might be the world's definition of heroes.
> In her book, they always would be.
>
> Anchoring, Problem, Run, Stakes

> Kacie Billings had waited half her life to get a glimpse of hell, to feel the heat blast from its core, taste the dry air parch her throat, hear the crackle as it chewed up the fuel behind the fireline. She'd grown up with pictures from her Catholic Bible embedded in her head, with stories from her Uncle Shep and the other firefighters churning in her thoughts. Fire fascinated her, hypnotized her, taunted her with its cunning.
> So she stood without fear on the bluff overlooking the Klondike Ravine framing in her viewfinder the five hotshots, with their green fire-retardant pants and yellow Nomex shirts, their red helmets, faces gritty and black with reverse raccoon eyes. She didn't think twice about the way the wind reached down and nipped her neck, a surprisingly cool bite after the scorching afternoon.
>
> Stakes, Heroine Identity

> Her father always said that one should never get too close to a sleeping dragon. But she had the perfect photo op, didn't she? Right here, on top of the Klondike Ravine, overlooking the scorched moonscape of the Lake Clark preserve, a 2.6 million acre swath of once lush hills, vibrant with color – green spruce, and purple lupine, red crowberries and white dwarf dogwoods -- now charred gray, skeletal trees stripped and fallen, the fallout of an late summer wildfire.   And in front of it all, five hearty hotshots, their faces gritty, red helmets layered in ash, grinned up at her, leaning on their pulaskis.
> "One more picture, guys!" She centered them in the viewfinder, ignoring the whip of wind that ran through her jacket.
> It was then the dragon awakened.
>
> Anchoring, Identity, Run

> The last snapshot Kacie Billings ever took was of Jeb Ransom, face sooty, eyes reddened with smoke, his blue handkerchief over his nose and mouth, his yellow shirt whipping into the wind as he deployed his fire shelter. Over her.
> While fire crested down on them in a tsunami of scorching death.
>
> Run, Stakes

Step Two: Create

> Kacie Billings didn't fear fire. She figured that perhaps once had been enough to satiate its ethereal hunger and that she possessed an immunity born from loss and grief, from the sacrifices of the generation before her. Fate, and fire, wouldn't want her.
>
> Which was why, on the south side of the Klondike Ravine, as the wall of fire rolled toward her, she stood frozen.
>
> Her Nikon dangling from her neck.
>
> Watching.
>
> Identity, Problem

And the (currently) winning hook:

> On a cool August day, on the south slope of the Klondike ravine in southern Alaska, Kacie Billings finally got her glimpse of hell.
>
> "One more picture, guys!" She centered her viewfinder on the five raccoon-eyed hotshots, all grinning up at her under their grimy red helmets, their flag-yellow Nomex shirts blazing through the haze. They leaned on their pulaskis as if they might be the world's definition of heroes.
>
> In her book, they were. Behind them, the scorched moonscape of the Lake Clark preserve, a 2.6 million acre swath of once lush hills, vibrant with color – green spruce and purple lupine, red crowberries and white dwarf dogwoods -- now charred gray, skeletal trees stripped and fallen, the fallout of a late summer wildfire.
>
> Perfect. Even, award-winning. See, with a little patience...
>
> She captured the shot, ignoring the whip of wind that ran through her jacket.
>
> That's when she heard the growl.
>
> And right behind it, the scream of fire boss Jed Ransom from along the ridge.
>
> *Run.*
>
> Anchoring, Problem, Run, Stakes, Heroine Identity

Keep in mind that the SHARP hook examples were all from the *first paragraph* of a novel. But you also want to keep hooks in mind for the first paragraph of *every new scene*. You don't want your reader to put your book down at the beginning of the next chapter, right? Just like the first paragraph, you need to consider how you will grab their attention at the beginning of each scene too.

Here are some quick ideas how to start those scenes:

- ✓ With dialogue.
- ✓ Describing a character who is new, yet essential, to the scene.
- ✓ Setting--especially to set mood.
- ✓ A narrative statement
- ✓ Action

Most importantly, start late, leave early! If your character is going somewhere, have them already pulling up, or inside the building. You can throw in a couple lines of narration to sum up what happened, but you want to focus the scenes on the action, not on the boring stuff of driving or getting dressed, or eating. (Unless, of course, that's an important part of the scene!)

Your Turn:

Stakes

Hero/Heroine Identification

Anchoring

Run

Problem/Story Question

Now, try your first hook !Highlight all the SHARP elements.

Now refine your hook and try again:

Yay! You have your first line! Now, keep it up for every chapter!

So, what else goes into a scene? After Storyworld and a SHARP hook, you need *someone* in the scene.

POV: Who's talking?

Why is point of view(POV) important, and how can it help or harm our work?

Point of View: What is it? It's the view or perspective of the protagonist or secondary characters. Another way to explain it is: the "story view" of the hero or the heroine.

First let's address overall POV choices.

There are several types of POV writing:

- Limited Third Person
- Omniscient,
- Narrative
- First Person
- Second Person

Now, some POV choices are made because of the author's strengths and weaknesses. Sometimes authors write in third person or first person because it's their best voice. Other times, it's about the best voice for the story. For example, private investigator (PI) books or women's fiction often have a first-person POV. No matter how the choice is made, however, there is always a POV character and it's his/her voice we hear throughout the book.

> **Limited third person** is the most popular POV used today. This means the story is being told through the eyes, ears, and mouth of one character at a time. The writer may have multiple characters "telling" the story, but only one is on stage, speaking, at a time.

Let's look at a romance. The hero and heroine usually have a POV in the story. The author will break up the story into scenes, describing the plot and action from one or the other's POV.

> Here's an example:

> Tom stood to watch the boats docking in the moor. The wind pressed the hem of his shirt against his abdomen as he raised his hand to shield his eyes from the sun. How could he be like one of the boats, free and out on the open sea? His mouth watered at the idea. His heart beat as if he'd actually cut and run.

Behind him, Rachel waited, feeling alone and left out.

Now, what's wrong with this example? I told you what *both* Tom and Rachel were feeling. That's called "head hopping"—when something is observed that the POV character can't think or experience. Want to convey someone else's thoughts in the scene? One idea would be for the POV Character to *guess* the attitudes or thoughts of the character's he's talking to, based on that character's body language , which then would affect the POV character's responses.

I read a book review where the reviewer referred to *changing POV* as head hopping. That's not head hopping. There's a difference between the two.

Changing POV for a new scene is a legitimate and necessary story too.l You changePOV by simply inserting a substantial line break, or perhaps asterisks, between the two POVs. Head hopping—telling the reader how two people in the same scene both feel—is not a legitimate story tool. It jerks the reader's emotions back and forth. Who do I feel for in the previous scene? Tom, who wants to be free of his burdens, or Rachel who feels left out and alone?

Let's rewrite the scene from Tom's POV:

Tom stood to watch the boats docking in the moor. The wind pressed the hem of his shirt against his abdomen as he raised his hand to shield his eyes from the sun. How could he be like one of the boats, free and out on the open sea? His mouth watered at the idea. His heart beat as if he'd actually cut and run.

"Tom, what you are doing? Let's go."

Tom looked back at Rachel. She stood by the car, arms crossed, frown on her face. She was mad, he guessed, but for the moment, he didn't care.

See the difference? We see the world and Rachel, only from Tom's POV. The reader cannot know anything Tom does not. To show conflict with Rachel, I added dialogue. She sounds impatient, doesn't she?

When Tom looks around, we "read" her through his eyes. We get the idea all is not well between them. We are sympathetic toward Tom. Our emotions are with him until, of course, we change to Rachel's POV and we see her side of the story.

You can show your characters' feelings and emotions in the story narrative, but another way is in dialogue followed by an action tag. This is an effective way to "show" the scene.

"Tom, what are you doing? Let's go." Rachel hammered the hood of the car with her fist.

Oh, now we really see her 'tude. So does Tom. We understand what he knows about Rachel.

> **Omniscient POV** is the "God voice." It's when the author is narrating the story from overhead, dipping into the minds of all the characters at once. However, sometimes it slips into a third person story. When it does, it's called "author intrusion." This

means the author has introduced facts and ideas the POV character does not know. The classic omniscient infraction is "little did he know . . . "

That phrase makes me laugh. Or, the author might pen, "Tomorrow, Rachel would wonder why she ever let Tom talk her into driving to the river."

In **First person POV** the story is told through the "I" of the protagonist. Usually there is only one POV character in first person books because the voice and sound is so unique. But you can tell a story with multiple POV characters if the voices are distinct enough.

I (Rachel) had two first person POVs in *Diva NashVegas*. When I wrote the hero, Scott's, dialogue, I tried really hard to make him sound like a dude, very distinct from my heroine, Aubrey.

A clear POV character in each scene is the key to building a strong story with solid writing. You can "head hop" if you want and tell us what everyone including the grocery store clerk is feeling or thinking, but it's confusing to the reader, and sign of lazy writing. Head hopping is also different from the slide into different POVs many romance writers use. They make an easy transition between POVs, but then establish themselves firmly in one POV at a time).

Choosing your POV character

When I talked with editors at Thomas Nelson, I learned they like third–person POV because of the versatility it provides. They felt that sometimes a first-person POV can become claustrophobic.

I didn't understand what they meant by "claustrophobic" until I read a first-person book where the story was so close to the protagonist, I felt locked in. I wanted to see beyond her, outside of her world. The way to accomplish this in first person POV is to:

   1. Add another POV.

   2. Add dialogue and scenes with other characters and broaden the landscape.

Which character should have the POV in a scene? With multiple POV characters, such as in a romance or suspense, how do you know which character should be on stage? Don't they both have something at stake? Who do we need to hear from? Who will be telling the story?

Answer : the one with the most *at stake.* The one whose goals and actions are the most affected by the scene and the conflicts therein. This doesn't mean the other members of the scene aren't affected, and in fact, the Action scene *should* lead to a ReAction scene for them.)

Again, write the scene from the POV of the character who would be impacted the most emotionally, or "who has the most to lose."

There are scenes, of course, where something happens that affects both characters equally. But there are ways to handle that. In *In Sheep's Clothing*, the prologue is in one character's POV, describing a scene that happens one-third of the way into the book. When I get to that scene, it is repeated in a different character's POV. Another way to see how a scene affects two characters is to have the secondary character rehash the scene, from their perspective, in a subsequent scene.

In romance, it's standard to have an equal amount of time "on stage" for the hero and heroine, though don't feel overly bound by this. Again, make your choice based on who can best tell the story.

In *Love Starts With Elle*, I (Rachel) had a scene where the hero returns to Elle's life. Originally, I told the story in her POV, but in my rewrites, I changed to the hero's POV. Ultimately, he had the most to lose.

If the story is suspense, perhaps the antagonist will have a few scenes. What are they plotting? How does it advance the story?

If a scene is dragging or feels flat, change the POV. Maybe even introduce a new character. I've done this for my first-person books because the protagonist was too introspective. So, I added a townsperson or a friend the heroine could talk to. It opened up the scene to experience it from a fresh view.

The bottom line: Choose the POV character that has the most at stake and who best moves the action forward.

Your Turn

Determine your POV voice: Take your main character and put him in a scene.

Write the scene from the first person POV.

Now try the scene from the third person POV.

Which seems stronger to you?

Multiple POV choice: Who else is in the scene?

Out of the lineup of cast members, who has the most at stake in the scene?

Who would react strongest to the situation, emotionally or physically?

What POV impacts readers the most?

Let's Talk: Dialogue!

Dialogue isn't just made up of words—it's also what is *not* being said. Dialogue is body language and internal monologue and, most of all, it's conflict. Dialogue more than anything moves a scene, creates emotion, reveals motivations, and produces change in a character. But good dialogue is difficult to write. Here's a hint: Dialogue is not conversation!

Good dialogue has four functions:

1. **Reveal characters** – Dialogue reveals a character, but only as much as they want to be revealed. It tells the kind of personality they are, how they feel about the people they're conversing with, where they're from, their education, profession, etc. Your reader should know who is speaking without any dialogue tags, i.e. *he said* or *she said*.

2. **Move plot** – Dialogue moves the story along by revealing information and raising new questions. If you want a fast scene, insert a lot of dialogue.

3. **Create Conflict** – Until you reach the Happily Ever After, dialogue should, even if it's not an argument, deepen the conflict between characters, create inner dissonance in the characters, and distance them from their plot goals. Even if it is a sweet, romantic scene, dialogue will make the characters long to be together, when we know they can't be. If they're perfect for each other, but the hero knows they can't be together, then that will create inner dissonance. Conflict drives a story, and we want lots of it!

4. **Illuminate or prepare characters for an epiphany** – Dialogue is a great device to lead the character into a deeper understanding of himself, and eventually lead to his epiphany moment. Tidbits of truth, dropped and revealed along the way, will be gathered like breadcrumbs to help him understand himself, and lead him to finally to his Aha! moment.

Conversation vs. Dialogue: What's the difference?

Conversation is what you and I have every day. Here are some recent snippets from our house:

> **Mom:** Hi honey, how was school?
>
> **Daughter:** Boring.
>
> **Mom:** Did anything exciting happen today?
>
> **Daughter:** No. What's for supper?
>
> **Mom:** Hotdogs.
>
> **Daughter:** Seriously?
>
> **Mom:** Seriously.
>
> **Daughter:** I have homework.

> Okay, not riveting stuff.

Most conversation happens about unimportant, everyday things. And it's boring. Good dialogue only *seems* like real speech. It's conversation with all the boring stuff deleted, leaving only the essential, the emotional, the most dramatic words.

GUSTO – Creating Great Dialogue

I want to talk to you."
"Hi, Maggy. How are you?"
"Don't 'how are you' me! I can't believe you came back to take away Cole's land."

Okay, I admit it. Dialogue is my favorite part of a book. I just love to hear people get into arguments, dodge questions, tell it like it is, and most of all, give each other what for. Sometimes (and this is the schizophrenic writer side of me) I will even talk out loud as I'm writing dialogue, just to get the inflection. I can also say anything to myself and not get into trouble!

But what is the secret to sizzling dialogue? What's the difference between writing conversations that zing and mind-numbing dialogue that causes a book to end face down on the bureau collecting dust?

I think it's all about adding a little **GUSTO**– the element that contains attitude and energy and courage and everything your character has inside of him.

What do I mean? Let's take a closer look:

Goals – Every character has goals for the scene, as well as for the book. And good dialogue reveals those goals—not only by what is being said, but what is *not* being said. Don't let your characters lay it all on the line. Make them hide their motives to everyone but the reader. In fact, don't even let them answer the questions they're asked. Dodge, be evasive, and most of all, never give the expected answer. Not if you don't want readers to skip lines.

Ask: What must my character accomplish in this chapter?

Ask: What feelings is he going to show? And, what doesn't my character want others to know about him?

Useful information – Dialogueshould give new information to the reader, but *don't* use it in place of backstory.Don't use dialogue to "inform" the reader:

"Joe, I know that you're the great uncle of my step-sister, Sally, and that you were having an affair secretly with my dad's ex-wife who left her and became an alcoholic and eventfully died after going to rehab for liver disease, and that you now got your life together and became a Christian after attending a Billy Graham event in Minneapolis four years ago, after which you dedicated your life to helping orphans in Russia, but could you tell me why my step-sister won't speak to my little brother, especially since they used to be so close, until he left for the navy two years ago and is in now in Navy Seal training because this was the dream of my father due to my grandfather who was one of the first SEALS in WW II?"

Make dialogue meaningful. Don't ask how anyone is, or how the family is, or how the weather is (unless it's a weather book). Cut right to the meat of the story with new information.

Stop Shouting! Don't use Tom Swifts – "Stop Shouting!" he yelled. "I'll tell you all about it," she explained. Use dialogue tags sparingly, and keep them to *he said*, *she said*, with the occasional *he murmured* or *she whispered*. In fact, body language and active narrative in place of dialogue tags speaks as loudly as words, if not louder.

Here are two scenes, one with just dialogue, one with added body language and narrative. Which one reveals more?

Example 1: "I don't care where you're going. Stay out all night if you want to. In fact, I hope you have a great time."

Example 2: "I don't care where you're going." Janice barely looked up from her book as her sister stood by the door, a question on her face. "Stay out all night if you want to." She put a thumb over the paragraph to keep her place. She looked up and smiled, a real smile that filled her chest and made her sister smile back. "In fact, I hope you have a great time."

Or, you could go another way:
"I don't care where you're going." Janice dumped the baked potatoes into the garbage. "Stay out all night if you want to." She flashed him a smile as she threw the casserole pan into the sink, turned on the water full blast. She forced herself not to wince as it splashed her face. "In fact, I hope you have a great time." She grabbed the towel and very, very slowly wiped her face, keeping the towel there until she heard the soft click of the door closing behind her husband.

Same words, different body movement, *much* different tone.

> **Tell it like it is** – Cut to the chase and say what your character *really* wants to say, even if it is only to take away attention from his real agenda. The best dialogue is when you think, "Oh my, I can't believe she (or he) had the guts to say that!"

"It's Noble land. But, Maggy, this isn't about you."

"This is completely about me, Nick. I know that! I'm not an idiot."

"Of course you're not. It's just that . . . this is between me and Cole."

"You think I don't know why you left? Why you haven't come back for ten years? You're really a piece of work, Noble. Well, for your information, Cole is twice the man you are. He's kind and honorable and patient, and he keeps his promises. He deserves that land your father gave him. And you, of all people, should know that."

"I don't know what you're talking about, Maggy, but you got this all wrong."

"You turned out exactly as my mother predicted. I'm so sorry I didn't listen to her sooner."
(Excerpted from *Reclaiming Nick*)

Don't overuse names – We writers use names to help us remember who's who when we're writing. But the reader doesn't need them, so cut them out as you're editing. For example:

"Hey Sam, how are you?"

"Hey Joe, I'm good, but my car is in the shop."

"Sam, your car is always in the shop."

" I know, Joe, but it's got a bad starter."

"Have you ever thought of getting it fixed, Sam?"

Have fun with your dialogue. Let your characters say what they really want to say, use body language for tags, and remember their goals and you'll have dialogue with umph!

> "I think this dialogue section is getting a little long," Rachel said just above a whisper to the My Book Therapy audience.
>
> Yeah, Susie could hear her, but really, did Rachel have to point out that she was long-winded? "So I have a lot to say about dialogue. It's my favorite part about writing. What's the big deal? It's probably the key to a great book, so just calm down, Florida Girl," Susie said with a huff.

How to handle Internal Monologue

What is Internal Monologue? Should I italicize my character's thoughts?

These are two questions I get —because a lot because, let's be honest, it's confusing. Frankly, every author seems to do it differently.

Here's my take: If you're in a character's POV, then every thought, action, feeling, etc, funnels through *their* brain. If it doesn't have quotation marks around it, it's their thoughts. You'd have to italicize the entire page!

Let's take a closer look:

I really don't want her to leave, because if she does leave I'll be alone and back where I started.

I think italicizing these thoughts is jarring for the reader, carrying less of an impact. If you're writing in third person, just write the character's thoughts in third person.

Try: *He didn't want her to leave. Not really. Because then where would he be?*

Do you see the difference? This allows the reader to sympathize with your character. In fact, the reader knows him better than your character knows himself at this point, which is fun for the reader.

The same goes for phrases like "he thought," or "he wondered." You know who is thinking the thought, so it's not necessary to use these words.

Did he really want her to leave? No, he thought.

Try: Did he really want her to leave? No.

> Not: He always took a good thing and tore it to pieces, he thought about himself.
>
> But: He always took a good thing and tore it to pieces.

And you can create even more impact by converting interior monologue into a question.

> Not: He wondered why he always took a good thing and tore it to pieces.
>
> Better: Why did he always take a good thing and tear it to pieces?

Hint: Limit your internal monologue to within the dialogue scene for the most punch. I really think that internal monologue in the middle of a narrative is confusing, even if it's in italics.

What about internal introspection? I sometimes use this during an epiphany, when a character is remembering something he or she said, or something someone said to them, but even then, I keep the memory in italics, and keep the introspection in thoughts.

Generally, if there is "screaming in my head," then I go with italics.

> Example: No! I thought, please don't go—
>
> Better: *No! Please don't -go—*

Let's sum up the differences:

Original bad-Susie writing:

> "I think this dialogue section is getting a little long," Rachel said just above a whisper to the MBT audience.
>
> *Yeah, I could hear her, but really, did Rachel have to point out that I am long-winded?* "So I have a lot to say about dialogue. It's my favorite part about writing—what's the

big deal? It's probably the key to a great book, so just calm down, Florida Girl," Susie said with a huff.

Cleaner:

"I think this dialogue section is getting a little long," Rachel said just above a whisper to the MBT audience.

Rachel was always pointing out that she was long-winded. "So I have a lot to say about dialogue. It's my favorite part about writing—what's the big deal? It's probably the key to a great book, so just calm down, Florida Girl," Susie said with a huff.

Better:

"I think this dialogue section is getting a little long," Rachel said just above a whisper to the MBT audience.

Why was Rachel always pointing out that she was long-winded? "So I have a lot to say about dialogue. It's my favorite part about writing—what's the big deal? It's probably the key to a great book, so just calm down, Florida Girl."

Best:

"I think this dialogue section is getting a little long," Rachel said just above a whisper to the MBT audience.

Yeah, Susie could hear her, but really, did Rachel always have to point out that she was long-winded? "So I have a lot to say about dialogue. It's my favorite part about writing—what's the big deal? It's probably the key to a great book, so just calm down, Florida Girl."

See how the voice gets stronger, less jarring, each time?

And here's a final caveat: Good internal monologue should be interspersed lightly, and be only the thoughts the POV character would think. Same goes with tone of voice—sparingly, but with impact. Your tone of voice is actually an extension of the thoughts, so often describing it isn't even necessary. Also, one of the fun parts of interspersing internal monologue is that your character can be saying one thing, and thinking something totally different. His tone of voice can also convey that.

Some last comments:
    He snarled.
    He muttered.
    He snapped.
    He growled.

But, please not:
    He laughed. (Not as a dialogue tag. Okay as a sentence.)
    He stammered. (You can write the stammering words instead.)
    He smiled. (Again, *not* a dialogue tag.)

But, I'll let you use, *he whispered*. Maybe. Once.

Just write *he said* or *she said*. And fill in the rest.

www.learnhowtowriteanovel.com

Super Secret Dialogue Hint:

I love *House*. (I'm talking about television now, not movies. This show, about a doctor, has just about the best dialogue on the planet. I love *House* because Dr. Gregory House (and other characters) says things that make me howl, stop the Tivo, and beat the sofa in hilarity.

Clearly, the writers of *House* have let their characters off their leashes, allowing them to say all sorts of crazy things, creating sparks that wows their audience.

Fighting words, I call them.

That is my super-secret Susie hint to writing great dialogue.

What are Fighting Words?

Interruptions: "Hey Susie, we don't have enough about dialogue—"
"Can't you see I'm in the middle of a paragraph here, Rachel?"

Name-calling: "Maybe you have snow on your brain, Ms. Northwoods."

Sarcasm: "Oh sure, because the sun doesn't actually make it all the way up here to the north, so it is a little difficult to see the difference in days and nights."

Accusations: "Good grief, Rachel, do you know how long it takes to warm my fingers up to type every morning?"

(Clarification: Okay, seriously, Rachel and I don't ever fight. *I totally made the last section up.* So, just in case you're thinking, "Wow, Rachel, totally get off her back already," or conversely, "Susie, sheesh, you're so sensitive,"—It's all fiction. In my head. Or rather now, forever in print . . . oh boy . . . .)

Back to Fighting words: In short, they are anything that makes the dialogue sound real (only not real, because like I said, no one really has the guts to say these things, or perhaps was raised with the social decorum to know that they shouldn't say these things to their best friend).

One helpful technique: Find the "hook" or the zinger in every sentence, and have the characters react to that, sort of like a snowball, getting more and more intense as it hurtles down the mountain.

"I don't feel like going to school today," Sarah said, the covers pulled up to her chin. I noticed, however, that her freshly applied mascara didn't bear at all the marks of overnight smudging.

"School? Where *do* you feel like going today, huh? Maybe the mall?"

Or:

"I don't feel like going to school today," Sarah said, pulling the covers over her head.

"Yeah, well I don't feel like going to work, either, but that's life. Deal with it."

See how I used two different hooks in each sentence, and gave each a different direction for the dialogue to go next.

But what if we don't have a big fight scene? How can we make that resonate?

You can create tension in any scene, you just have to dig for it. Let's take a normal conversation, but wrap it up in opposing goals. Let's take the dialogue from the Internal Monologue section (Last time, I promise!):

"I think this dialogue section is getting a little long," Rachel said just above a whisper to the MBT audience.

Yeah, Susie could hear her, but really, did Rachel always have to point out that she was long-winded? "So I have a lot to say about dialogue. It's my favorite part about writing—what's the big deal? It's probably the key to a great book, so just calm down, Florida Girl."

Can you find the zingers? There are two, possibly three, depending on whether you count Rachel's POV.

Accusation – Rachel
Sarcasm – Susie
Name calling – Susie

Fighting words don't have to be used in *every* conversation, but they add spice, and hopefully make your readers howl with delight. So, don't forget them Fighting Words!

Your Turn

Pick a scene with dialogue to work on:

What do the characters in the scene each need to accomplish, and what emotions will they be showing?

What do they really want to say? Don't go with your first instinct. Write their true emotions.

What is the one tone of voice you could insert that would add impact?

What action could they be doing that accentuates their words? What is the appropriate body language for their attitude? What could they be hiding?

What fighting words come to mind you could insert?

So, let's recap before we move on to what I call EXTRAS

How do we write a scene?

Determine **Action or ReAction** – Figure out if you're writing an action or a reaction and define your goals, conflict, disaster, or your response, dilemma, decision.

Create **Storyworld** using the NEWS and the Five Senses
–Mood – Pick your setting and the mood you want to convey.

Find your opening **Sentence/Hook** – Reveal your character's goals and bring the reader instantly into the scene.

Determine who is your **POV Character** – Stay in your POV character's head. Don't wander into the other characters' POV.

Fine tune **Dialogue** – What will your character try and accomplish? What will he talk about?

Give your POV character some Action or –Movement – Give him something tangible to do in the scene, some activity that is related to his goal. Or maybe it's an internal goal, and this is just a background activity.

Now, close your eyes, and walk into the scene with your hero. Let him open his mouth and speak, letting the scene unravel to the disaster or decision. If you, as a writer are there, your reader will be also.

Step Three: Publish

I hope by the time you've turned to this section, you have at least the first chapter done. If not, put this book down right now and go back and write. Right now. *Do it.* I don't want to see you again until you have at least 1500 words of your WIP saved in your "First Chapter of My Amazing Book" file.

All right, now that you have something to work with, let's talk about editing. See, you can't edit something that *isn't there*. Think of editing as taking that rough form and making a masterpiece out of it.

Now, as I mentioned before, I like to get it all on the page and write the entire book before I edit. Some authors, however, like to edit as they go. But be warned: You can really get caught up in editing. It's easier, in some ways, than writing, because the words are already there. You don't have to create. So, make some limits for yourself. Do only one or two editing passes before you force yourself to keep going. You can always come back later and re-edit. If you edit after you're farther in the story, you'll discover new elements and textures you want to add to your previous chapters.

Editing

Editing, in my opinion, is the fun part of writing. You already have the rough draft nailed down, and now you're going to hone it, add all those things that will make it sparkle.

For me, there are three phases to writing a book:

1. **Creating** – The long, painful discovery of the scenes. Again, keep a notebook of all the things you want to put in it later during the:

2. **Revision phase** – It's the phase where I hone the theme and add special elements, like the five senses, or thematic metaphors. I draw out scenes that need to be longer, shorten ones that are too long, even delete unnecessary scenes. This is where I add character textures such as:
   - ✓ *Idiosyncrasies – mannerisms, something the character says out of habit.*
   - ✓ *Food and drink preferences*
   - ✓ *Clothing and kind of car*
   - ✓ *Nicknames (my secret weapon)*

   Which leads us to the:

3. **Editing phase** – Print your scene out and read it slowly, taking notes in the lines, proofing it, and going through my checklist.(See below.)

Editing Checklist:

What to look for when editing:

- ✓ **Scenes that pack a punch** – Do each of your scenes have a purpose? Do you need to make the slower scenes faster? Can you combine two slow scenes, cutting away the less important to the important?
- ✓ **Action** – Are there sufficient reasons for everything your character does in that scene? Have you planted the clues for that action or decision long before they do it?
- ✓ **Likeable characters** – Does your hero/heroine have great qualities that make you truly like them? Make sure that in each scene, there is something likeable about your character—that special spark that sets them apart.
- ✓ **Surprise** – Is the disappointment worthy of your character? Is it plausible *and* unexpected?

✓ **Art** – Have you mastered the mechanics?

Mechanics Overview

1. Are there five senses in each scene?

2. Replace the adverbs with strong verbs, the adjectives with defined nouns. Cut all "ly" ending adverbs if possible.

3. Be ruthless with passive sentences. – "Was" and "were" are good clues to a passive sentence. Although sometimes you need a passive sentence to let the reader rest, most of your sentences should be active.

4. Repeating sentences – If two sentences say virtually the same thing, cut one.

5. Two adjectives together weaken both. Use the strongest one.

6. Read through your dialogue – Do you need tags? Do you have enough action between words? Do you repeat names? Do you need to delete tags to make it faster? Is there enough white space between chunks of dialogue? Body language? Fighting words?

7. Do you have a list of overused words? Do a word search and fix/delete those!

Now, what is the difference between *strengthening* a scene and *re-arranging* the words?

Strengthening a scene is discovering the emotional significance to the scene, the way it will affect the overall book, and milking it for the reader. Using setting and dialogue and body language and disappointment and *words* to cut to the heart of a character.

Rearranging words, on the other hand, is merely putting them in a different order. Ordering them differently. Rearranging them so they say that same thing, only in a different way. Maybe even going on and on and on about the same thing in hopes of driving your point home . . . .

Let's take a look at the editing process in an actual scene. Below are three excerpts: the original, the edit, and the final product. See if you can see how I applied my editing checklist to strengthen the scene. This is the prologue from *In Sheep's Clothing*.

Prologue

Five more minutes and she would be safe.

Gracie Benson hunched her shoulders and pulled the woolly brown scarf over her forehead, praying desperately her guise as a Russian peasant worked. Fear roiled through her as the train engine thundered through the station. She bristled, watching an elderly gentleman gather his bags, two canvas duffels, and shuffle across the cement platform. Would he turn, and scream, "Foreigner!" in the tongue that now drove fear into her American bones?

Without a glance at her, he joined the throng of other passengers moving toward the train as it rumbled by, one forest-green colored wagon after another. Another man, dressed upscale in a three-piece black silk suit fell in behind him. Gracie stiffened. Did he glance her way? <u>Help me, Lord</u>!

She didn't know whom to trust after this morning's horrific events.

The train slowed, ground to a stop, and hissed. Gracie shuffled forward, in keeping with her disguise of tired village maiden. She clutched a worn nylon bag in one –hand—her black satchel safely tucked –inside—and fisted the folds of her headscarf with the other. The smell of diesel fuel and dust hovered over the platform like a fog. Cries of good-bye drifted from well-wishing relatives, for others more fortunate and less alone than she.

Casting a furtive glance beyond the crowd, she caught sight of a militia officer. Fear coiled in her stomach. The soldier, dressed in muddy green fatigues, had an AK-47 hung over his shoulder like a fishing basket, and leaned lazily against the entrance doors, paying her no mind.

Hope lit inside her. Freedom beckoned from the open train door.

Stepping up to the conductor, she handed the woman her wadded ticket. The conductor glared at her as she unfolded the slip of paper. Gracie dropped her gaze and acted servile, her heart in her throat. The conductor paused only a moment before punching the ticket and motioning for Gracie to enter.

Gracie hauled up her jean skirt and climbed aboard.

The train smelled of hot vinyl and aged wood. The body odor of previous passengers clung to the walls, and grime pooled along the edges of a brown linoleum floor. Gracie bumped along the narrow corridor until she found her compartment. She'd purchased the entire private berth with the intent of slamming the door, locking it from inside, and not cracking it open until she reached Vladivostok. The U.S. Consulate, only ten minutes from the train station, meant safety and escape from the nightmare.

Surely Evelyn's assassin wouldn't follow her to America.

Prologue with edits

If the train trudged any slower into the station, American missionary Gracie Benson would be dead by sunset. Five minutes. Twenty steps. Then she'd be safely aboard.

God obviously wasn't on her side. Not today, at least.

Then again, He certainly didn't owe her any favors. Not after her fruitless two years serving as a missionary in Russia.

Gracie purposely kept her gaze off heaven as she ~~Five more minutes and she would be safe.~~

~~Gracie Benson~~ hunched her shoulders and pulled the woolly brown scarf over her forehead. ~~,~~ Please, *please* let her guise as a Russian peasant work. ~~praying desperately her guise as a Russian peasant worked.~~ The train huffed its last, then belched, and Gracie jumped. *Hold it together, Grace.* Long enough to fool the conductor, and find her berth on the train for Vladivostok. ~~Fear roiled through her as the train engine thundered through the station.~~ Then she could finally slam the compartment door on this horrific day—no, on this entire abysmal chapter of her dark life. So much for finding redemption as a missionary in Russia. She'd settle for getting out of the country alive.

She tensed ~~bristled~~, watching an elderly man dressed in the ancient Russian garb of worn fake leather jacket, wool pants, and a fraying beret, ~~gentleman~~ gather his bags, two canvas duffels, and shuffle across the cement platform. Would he turn, and scream, "Foreigner!" in the tongue that now drove fear into her American bones?

Without a glance at her, he joined the throng of other passengers moving toward the train as it rumbled by, one forest-green colored wagon after another. Another man, dressed mafia-style in a crisp black leather jacket and suit pants, ~~upscale in a three-piece black silk suit~~ fell in behind him. Gracie stiffened. Did he glance her way? *Help me, Lord*!

Just because God wasn't listening didn't mean she couldn't ask. The irony pricked her eyes with tears. This morning's events had whittled down her list of trustworthy souls in Russia to a fine point. She'd give all the rubles in her pocket for someone like her cousin, Chet, FBI agent extraordinaire, to yank her out of this nightmare into safety.

Not that she would give any man a chance to introduce himself before decking him. She'd been down that road once. Never was too soon to trust another man within arm's distance.

~~She didn't know whom to trust after this morning's horrific events.~~

~~The train slowed, ground to a stop, and hissed.~~ Gracie shuffled forward, in keeping with her disguise of tired village maiden. She clutched a worn nylon bag in one -hand—her black satchel safely tucked -inside—and fisted the folds of her headscarf with the other. The smell of diesel fuel and dust soured the breathable air and cries of good-bye ~~The smell of diesel fuel and dust hovered over the platform like a fog. Cries of goodbye drifted from well-wishing relatives, for others more fortunate and less alone than she.~~ from well-wishing relatives pooled grief in Gracie's chest.

Poor Evelyn.

Biting back grief, Gracie cast ~~Casting~~ a furtive glance beyond the crowd **and**~~, she~~ caught sight of a militia officer. ~~Fear coiled in her stomach.~~ The soldier, dressed in muddy green fatigues, had an AK-47 hung over his shoulder like a fishing basket, and leaned lazily against the entrance doors, paying her no mind.

Hope lit inside her. Freedom beckoned from the open train door.

Stepping up to the conductor, she handed the woman her wadded ticket. The conductor glared at her as she unfolded the slip of paper. Gracie dropped her gaze and acted servile, her heart in her throat. ***Please, please.*** The conductor paused only a moment before punching the ticket and **moving aside** ~~motioning for Gracie to enter~~.

~~Gracie hauled up her jean skirt and climbed aboard.~~

The train resonated with age in the smell of hot vinyl and polished wood. ~~The train smelled of hot vinyl and aged wood.~~ The body odor of previous passengers clung to the walls, and grime pooled along the edges of a brown linoleum floor. Gracie bumped along the narrow corridor until she found her compartment. She'd purchased the entire private berth with the intent of slamming the door, locking it from inside and not cracking it open until she reached Vladivostok. The U.S. Consulate, only ten minutes from the train station, meant safety and escape from the nightmare.

~~Surely Evelyn's assassin wouldn't follow her to America.~~

Escape from the memories. Surely Evelyn's killer wouldn't follow Gracie to America.

Final Prologue

If the train trudged any slower into the station, American missionary Gracie Benson would be dead by sunset. Five minutes. Twenty steps. Then she'd be safely aboard.

God obviously wasn't on her side. Not today, at least.

Then again, He certainly didn't owe her any favors. Not after her fruitless two years serving as a missionary in Russia.

Gracie purposely kept her gaze off heaven as she hunched her shoulders and pulled the woolly brown scarf over her forehead. Please, *please* let her guise as a Russian peasant work. The train huffed its last, then belched, and Gracie jumped. *Hold it together, Grace.* Long enough to fool the conductor and find her berth on the train for Vladivostok. Then she could finally slam the compartment door on this horrific day—no, on this entire abysmal chapter of her dark life. So much for finding redemption as a missionary in Russia. She'd settle for getting out of the country alive.

She tensed, watching an elderly man dressed in the ancient Russian garb of worn fake leather jacket, wool pants, and a fraying beret, gather his two canvas duffels and shuffle across the cement platform. Would he recognize her and scream, "Foreigner!" in the tongue that now drove fear into her American bones?

Without a glance at her, he joined the throng of other passengers moving toward the forest-green passenger cars. A younger man, dressed mafia-style in a crisp black leather jacket and suit pants, fell in behind the old man. Gracie stiffened. Did he look her way? *Help me, Lord!*

Just because God wasn't listening didn't mean she couldn't ask. The irony pricked her eyes with tears. This morning's events had whittled down her list of trustworthy souls in Russia to a fine point. She'd give all the rubles in her pocket for someone like her cousin, Chet, FBI agent extraordinaire, to yank her out of this nightmare into safety.

Not that she would give any man a chance to introduce himself before decking him. She'd been down that road once. Never was too soon to trust another man within arm's distance.

Gracie shuffled forward, in keeping with her disguise of tired village maiden. She clutched a worn nylon bag in one –hand—her black satchel safely tucked –inside—and fisted the folds of her headscarf with the other. The smell of diesel fuel and dust soured the breathable air and cries of good-bye from well-wishing relatives pooled grief in Gracie's chest.

Poor Evelyn.

Biting back grief, Gracie cast a furtive glance beyond the crowd and caught sight of a militia officer. The soldier, dressed in muddy green fatigues, hung an AK-47 hung over his shoulder like a fishing basket, and leaned lazily against a cement column, paying her no mind.

Hope lit inside her. Freedom beckoned from the open train door.

Stepping up to the conductor, she handed the woman her wadded ticket. The conductor glared at her as she unfolded the slip of paper. Gracie dropped her gaze and acted servile, her heart in her throat. *Please, please.* The conductor paused only a moment before punching the ticket and moving aside.

The train resonated with age in the smell of hot vinyl and polished wood. The body odor of previous passengers clung to the walls, and grime crusted the edges of a brown linoleum floor. Gracie bumped along the narrow corridor until she found her compartment. She'd purchased the private berth with the intent of slamming the door, locking it from inside and not cracking it open until she reached Vladivostok. The U.S. Consulate, only ten minutes from the train station, meant safety and escape from the nightmare.

Escape from the memories. Surely Evelyn's killer wouldn't follow Gracie to America.

Of course, there are entire books written on editing, the best being *Self-Editing for Fiction Writers* by Renni Browne and Dave King. Get it, study it, and edit your book to greatness!

"I saw the angel in the marble and carved until I set him free."

Michelangelo

Putting It All Together: Writing the Synopsis

So, you've written your book, edited it, and now, it's time to send the book in!

Okay, wait, maybe that proclamation was premature. I got a little excited there. First you need to write a Proposal, which consists of a cover or query letter (depending on what your prospective publisher wants to see first), a synopsis, and the first three chapters of your novel.

I like to write my cover or query letter *last*, because, well, by then I know what I'm trying to say.

And, you should already have those first three chapters written, right? (Because, well, you've also typed, "The End.")

So, let's talk a little about the **synopsis**.

We've talked about all the elements you'll need for your story: your physical, emotional, and spiritual plots, including the Black Moment and the epiphany. You know who your character is, what his values are, what motivates him and what his greatest dream is. Now, it's time to tell the world.

A synopsis is nothing more than a summary of your story. Go back to the Discover phase and remember your premise. Start with that, then use the following steps to weave these threads into a synopsis.

> **Step One:** A good synopsis starts out with outlining the character's deepest desires. What are they after, and why? What is God going to teach them? What are their motivations for these desires? What is their conflict?

> **Step Two:** Move the story through the obstacles. Highlight some of the things that your character will struggle with, spiritually and emotionally. Use the physical plot points to jump from paragraph to paragraph, writing it in proper POV.

> Note: A synopsis is supposed to be an **Overview** of the story. One mistake I see in beginning writers is the tendency to narrow in on the details. You want to step back from the story and squint a little and tell us the big events you see, and how they affect the spiritual and emotional threads. Don't tell us how he stops and caresses her hand as he declares his love. Just say, "He declares his love." Details slow the pace and will make the editor put the synopsis down. You don't want this to happen.

Hook your editor and bring him/her through the story, holding her breath, until you end with:

> **Step Three:** Is the theme verse or phrase pasted on the top of your computer. (Remember when I told you to do that? I told you we'd use it!) Tie up the synopsis

nicely by telling us how the theme fits in to your story, wrapping it up like a gift for your reader.

Don't worry about length, or style, just spit it out. We're not looking for a polished piece yet. You just want to tell the story. Shoot for three-five pages, and stick to the main plot. Your goal is to wind all the threads through the story, beginning to end. For now, just get it down on paper.

But what about those chapter–by-chapter summaries? Yes, there are a few publishers who want a chapter break-down. Don't panic. This is similar to a synopsis in that it includes desires, obstacles, and conflicts. It simply breaks them apart for each chapter.

Here's a secret: I often write both a synopsis and a chapter-by-chapter summary, even if my publisher only asks for one of them. I find the chapter-by-chapter summary serves as a roadmap for my book, and when I sit down to write it, I have a jumpstart on my creativity for that chapter. A synopsis is more entertaining, and a good way to introduce your writing style to your editor. But a chapter-by-chapter summary is more detailed, and proves you have your plot figured out. My suggestion: Try writing both!

The Knockout Punch!

Or: How to deliver a knock-out first paragraph.

Just like the first line of your book, you want the first paragraph of your synopsis to really grab your editor. You want to zero in on the most important parts of your book and hook them good. Because, although you are going to try and make your synopsis as entertaining as possible, it is still a summary. Therefore, you want to make sure you have the editor's interest before things slow down.

The Knockout Punch boils down the most important aspects of your story, the biggest interest-catcher, into a short paragraph.

Remember your premise? Go back and paste it at the top of your synopsis. There you go— Knockout!

When an editor is looking at your story, they want to know that you *know* what you're talking about. That you have it all "tied up." Nothing proves this more than having a knockout punch in the synopsis.

See, wasn't that easy? Now, let's keep going and write the REST of the synopsis!

Make It Colorful

A synopsis is not only the summary of your story. Like I said, it is a slice of your writing style. It gives the editor the first taste of who you are and what you write. Because of that, you want to give the synopsis the flavor of the type of story you write.

What do I mean? Well, we talked about how every noun and verb you use conveys a feeling or mood in a scene. For example, if you are trying to up tension and create fear, you might use verbs that generate feelings of fear. E.g., *stricken, caught, blindsided, choked.*

If you want to convey feelings of warmth, you might use *embraced, soothe, coo.* If you want to create feelings of suspense, you might use *flicker, ripped, tear.*

The idea is to look at your manuscript, and handpick the words you use to convey the mood and to illuminate the story. Then, use them when writing your synopsis. Why not? You want to create a mood for your synopsis, too, right?

Here are the first three paragraphs of the synopsis for my Deep Haven book, *The Perfect Match*. It is about the sparks that fly when the new lady fire chief falls for the town pastor. Let's start with the basic synopsis, without the colorful words.

> Ellie Karlson really wants to be a good firefighter. She's found a job in a small town and if she does really well, she'll not only be the permanent chief, but she'll also feel like she's somehow made up for causing the death of her brother. What she doesn't know is that there is someone setting fires in town and she'll have to catch him if she wants to keep her job. The lessons she learns about God in the process will change her life.

> Dan Matthews is tired of ministry. He needs help. But who can he look to? He desires a wife, but doesn't know the kind of wife God wants for him. On the night when one of his parishioners dies, he meets the new first chief, Ellie Karlson, and starts to wonder if she is the one God picked out. Can he sense God's will?

These paragraphs tell the basics, why Ellie wants to succeed, why Dan wants a wife. However, they doesn't have spark and sizzle.

Now, here's the synopsis with the color words added. I'm going to bold the words I use to convey mood.

> Ellie Karlson just **landed** her dream job . . . or so she thinks. In town to **helm** the three-month interim position of Fire Chief for the Deep Haven volunteer fire department, she has big plans to turn this into a permanent gig. It's taken fifteen years to finally fill the shoes her brother left behind with his untimely death, and she isn't going to let prejudice, an arsonist, or the chauvinistic town pastor keep her from her goals. But the job she's **sacrificed** for is about to **cost** more than she expects. Only by turning to God and **holding on tight** will she **survive**.

> Pastor Dan Matthews is feeling **burned out** in ministry. After three years at the helm of Grace Church in Deep Haven, he has serious **doubts** that his preaching or his attempts at discipleship are **bearing fruit** in the spiritual landscape of his congregation. Feeling like a failure, he can't help but wonder if firefighting is a better job. At least it has instant results. Maybe

what he needs is a partner –in ministry—a wife, a helper, just as God designed to **ease the load**. On the night when all his losses seem to **flash over**, he meet woman who can only be from hishis dreams, and he can't help but wonder if God has heard his silent prayers.

Then the smoke clears. Ellie Karlson may be a cute **fireball of energy**, but she's certainly not his picture of a helpmeet. She may be able to **haul hose** faster than any man in town, and know how to **chop down** a door with an axe, but last time he looked, those abilities weren't on his "perfect wife" qualifications. If only she didn't **light his heart on fire and ignite**, for the first time, the missing passion in his soul for life and ministry.

Your Turn:

Go through your synopsis and for each verb or noun, see if you can rework or find a way to make it stronger, add mood and give it punch.

Look for the Highlights!

When I first started writing a synopsis, it felt so *overwhelming*. Weaving in all those threads, and helping my editor see the main plot, as well as wondering whether I'd sufficiently explained all the turning points and the Black Moment . . . arrgh!

For example, running through your synopsis, you should have three different story threads: a spiritual thread, an emotional thread, and a plot thread. You should, in your first paragraphs, have outlined the beginning of these threads, and then through the subsequent paragraphs, be unrolling those threads.

In my synopsis about Mona and Joe (*Happily Ever After*), I start out with Mona's desires to start a bookstore and find her dream man, a book character named "Jonah." I also mention her greatest need: forgiveness. In the next paragraph, I mention her first obstacles in the plot.

Then I introduce the hero. Then I use a short paragraph to tell about Joe and his needs.

In the next paragraph, I return to the plot obstacles and throw in the spiritual obstacle from Mona's POV.

The next paragraph is about Joe, his issues, and a bit more of the emotional plot.

The idea I'm trying to get across (and you can read the entire synopsis in a moment), is that although you are unraveling the threads, you're not doing it evenly through the story, but in a way that adds *interest* and *punch*.

So, when you are all done, how do you *know* that the threads are all wound through the story, and tied up neatly? I came up with a handy-dandy trick to help me see my story as a whole and determine if there are any loose ends.

The Book Therapy Synopsis Trick:

After I've written my knockout punch and added colorful words through the synopsis, I print it out, find **three** different color highlighters, and sit down on the sofa with the piece.

I designate one color per thread and then, starting at the top of the synopsis, I read *only* for the spiritual thread, highlighting any sentences or thoughts that have to do with this thread. (Including the characters' desires/greatest needs.) I work my way through every page all the way to the end with just one color.

Then, I do the same for the emotional thread, and the plot thread. When I'm finished, I have a colorful (and smelly!) synopsis. However, *now* I can sit down with a pen and read through each thread individually, making sure it is complete. If I have holes, I just fill them in. I also look for redundancy. Have I said the same thing twice, or three times?

This little technique has helped eliminate editor (and personal) confusion, and made me feel confident that I am leaving no thread untied when I send in the story.

I know it sounds simple. That's the beauty of it! But it works.

Your Turn:

Find three different colors of highlighters. For each thread, read through the synopsis and highlight the physical, emotional, and spiritual threads, making sure they are complete and tied up.

(*Happily Ever After* synopsiss to paragraph four for your reference)
Synopsis - *Happily Ever After*
Susan M. Warren
Contemporary Romance
90,000+ words

Mona Reynolds has one dream: to open The Footstep of Heaven Bookstore and Coffee Shop in the enchanting tourist town of Deep Haven, Minnesota, and live out the little bit of heaven she and her father had dreamed about. To add to that dream a man who could love her unconditionally, the way her father did, is just too much to ask of God. All she wants is to open her bookstore and live in her memories.

But the Victorian house, which will be The Footstep of Heaven Bookstore, is riddled with problems from the first moment. Minor repairs sprout like weeds, and Mona and her partner, a potter named Liza Beaumont, are desperately in need of a handyman. Enter Joe Michaels. Ruggedly handsome in his faded Levis, Joe appears in his beat-up Ford, with a dog named Rip, and offers to fix everything.

But Joe has mending to do in his own life, namely a fraying relationship with his younger brother Gabriel, who lives in a group home not far from Deep Haven. Gabriel Michaels has Down syndrome, and Joe has returned from exploring the world to discover a brother he never knew.

Joe, Mona, and Liza set about repairing the house in time for the tourist season, only three months away. Despite Joe's skills and Mona's resourcefulness, disaster continues to assault them, from a flooded basement to an extended family of roaches. Mona realizes, as she watches her dreams (not to mention her life savings) erode, that she cannot create "heaven" on earth, nor find the peace she had before her father's death—a death that she caused.

Joe suspects there is something sinister behind Mona's inexhaustible repairs, and that something has to do with Brian Whitney, the building inspector for the county. Brian is a formidable foe: debonair and wielding the power to keep business doors closed. His somewhat annoying interest in both Mona and Liza has Joe suspicious—or is he jealous?

Query Letters

Now that you are tying up your threads for your synopsis and packing it with a punch, you only have two more aspects of your proposal to put together: your query letter and sample chapters.

A query letter may be sent separately, before you send in your entire proposal, or it may take the form of a cover letter. It can be sent via e-mail or hard copy. Always check to make sure your intended recipient—agent or editor—accepts e-mail queries.A query letter is your pitch...the what, why, and hows of your story.

What makes a good query letter?
1. A compelling, succinct first paragraph hook (aka, premise).
2. A summary of your book in two to three sentences.
3. An explanation of where your manuscript fits into the publishing world.
4. Who you are and why you can successfully pull off this book.
5. The mechanics of the –manuscript—where you're at in production.

The Hook:
In my opinion, the most important part of the query letter is the beginning hook. This is where you get the editor's attention, the part that will keep him/her from tossing all your hard work into the circular file. Consider how many proposals channel through an editor's hands in one month and this thought alone should impress you with the importance of the hook.

1. What is a hook?
It's the Who, What, and Why of the story. It's the juiciest tidbit, the selling aspect that makes *your* story different from the rest. This is where you take your knockout paragraph, boil it down to the *most* important aspect, and highlight it. You want to create questions and interest. You should do this in less than 100 words.

For example, in my query letter for *Happily Ever After*, I wrote:

Mona Reynolds longs for two things: forgiveness and Jonah, the hero from her favorite book. But getting either is about as likely as her father rising from the dead. Instead, she runs home, to Deep Haven, MN, to open her dream bookstore. Joe Michaels has never stopped running. He is merely slowing down to visit a brother he barely knows. When Mona's dreams begin to crumple, Joe is conveniently there to save her. But when dreams turn to disaster, is Joe the man she hopes he is? Or is he someone much, much different?

The key here is to *not* give away the details, but to think like a marketing person and find the juiciest tidbits. Think of the blurbs on the back of books. They grab you, and much of the time, based on that 100 word summary, you purchase the book. That is the response you're aiming for.

2. Summarizing your book.
What are the theme and the take-away message of your book? You must get very creative, descriptive, and frugal in this section of your query letter. The key is to say as much as

possible about the book, in terms of its content, in two to four sentences. Query letters should be one page only. The editor just doesn't have time to read more than that.

Here is what I wrote for *Happily Ever After*:

Through a myriad of disasters, including a family of roaches, a house fire, a saboteur, and finally the unveiling of Joe's secrets, Joe and Mona discover that when they turn their hopes over to the Lord, He will satisfy their wildest dreams and fulfill the longings of their hearts.

3. Where does your book fit in the market?

Is your book a stand alone? The first in a series? Why is it unique? This is the paragraph where you really sell your book. Go ahead, tell the editor why it is great, and tell him/her where it will fit in their lineup. Definitely do some research and know what the publisher offers. DON'T try and sell a romance to a publisher who doesn't publish romance. Then, pump up those traits your book has, the ones you know they want.

Here is my marketing paragraph. Note that I am selling the series, as well as book one.

Set in the fictional, picturesque tourist town of Deep Haven, northern Minnesota, *Happily Ever After* is the first in a three-part collection entitled, "The Deep Haven Series." Each book tells the story of a woman, running from the storms of life and searching for a home, who discovers true love and the inner peace that only a deep relationship with God can bring. The series combines the threads of mystery, suspense, and spiritual searching with heartwarming tales of love, and weaves them into satisfying romances set it in a town we'd all love to visit. Attached is a short summary of the series and the titles in the collection.

4. Who are you and why can you write this book?

In one or two sentences, highlight your publishing credits. If you don't have any, list the reasons why you are an authority to write this story. Obviously, I could pull off Russian stories with some degree of authenticity because of my missionary experience. And my first book with Tyndale was a "found my true love in Russia" story. I spent my childhood in an idyllic town in northern Minnesota, so I was able to write with some legitimacy about the state's north shore.

Here's my authority statement:

I am a missionary in Far East Russia, who grew up on the beautiful north shore of Minnesota. I've published numerous devotionals and articles, and this story won first place in an online contest.

5. The mechanics.

This paragraph simply explains how long the book is, how much you have written, whether your proposal is out to other publishers as well, and details the items you've included in your package. And, of course, don't forget to thank the editor for his or her time in reading the proposal.

Here's how I finished my query letter:

Happily Ever After is a completed manuscript of 90,000 words. Currently, this is a simultaneous submission. (Note: "Simultaneous submission" means you've sent the manuscript to other editors/agents at the same time. Check your publisher/agents policy on this. Attached please find the story synopsis and the first three chapters. Thank you for your consideration.

Those are the basics of a good query letter.

In short, the query letter hooks your editor on your idea and the synopsis hooks them on your ability to weave a story. And, of course, the sample chapters hook them on your writing ability.

Your Turn:

Let's break your query letter down into the essential pieces:

Hook

Summary

Marketability

Who/Why

Mechanics

A Word About Sample Chapters

Your proposal is nearly finished! You have your well-threaded synopsis, knockout first paragraph, and a compelling query letter that hooks your editor. Now, all you need are the sample chapters!

Sample Chapters:
Every proposal package includes sample chapters for the story you are proposing. Even if you are a multi-published author, you will have to write sample chapters for new contracts with new publishers, so it is wise to learn how to write them now.

When new authors read "Sample Chapters" in the submission requirements of an editor or publisher's website, sometimes they are tempted to think,"I'll pick my *best* chapters: chapter one, chapter eight, and chapter twenty-two." Delete that thought. Editor's *do not* want to see a set of random chapters. They want to see the *first three chapters*. They want to see how the story flows, they want to hear your voice, and they want to know how you develop characters. So, when you see the words "Sample Chapters," think: first three chapters. If you have a *short* prologue, you can include it. If, however, you have a prologue that is five pages long (and really, you shouldn't, but that's another discussion), include it as one of your first three chapters.

We've talked at length about writing your chapters, especially the beginning chapter. And, if you have followed the Lindy Hop Plot structure, by chapter three, your hero should be setting out on his Noble Quest. You've built in the Story Question, introduced your hero's goals, immersed him in Storyworld, tightened your writing, made it colorful—all with the hopes that you've stirred enough interest for the editor/agent to ask for the *full manuscript*! Think of the synopsis as your editor's first introduction to your writing, the teaser, so to speak. The sample chapters make them fall in love with your style.

When you prepare your sample chapters, refer to the publisher's guidelines to know how to format it. Some want a specific type style and margins. Always put a header on the top left with your name and the name of the manuscript. Add the page number in upper right hand corner.

I usually spend at least two weeks on my sample chapters, making sure they are compelling, introduce enough conflict, and make the editor want to turn the page. It pays to take the time to get it right, so don't rush it. Usually a good proposal takes me a month. One week for market research, another two for sample chapter polish,and one more for synopsis and query polish. Don't rush it. Once an editor reviews your work, if he or she turns it down, it is hard to get a second chance.

Writing is not a profession, occupation or job; it is not a way of life. It is a comprehensive response to life.

Gregory McDonald

The Writing Career

The writer's life is at once exciting and lonely. No one else is inside your brain with you as you create. No one else feels the same triumph when you get the scene right, or when your characters are finally overcoming their trials. I have a friend who calls me and occasionally she'll hear a long silence and know that I'm in the middle of a big scene. She's a good enough friend to say,"Uh, I'll call you later."

Getting your career started takes time and sometimes more energy than you have to offer. Whether you are a stay-at-home mom or a man working full time, or vice-versa, you'll struggle with carving out time. I was a home-schooling mom, and I really struggled sometimes with the balance between my kids' needs and my creative ideas running away with me.

Which brings me to a few hints about the life of a career writer.

Hints to developing a writing career:

- ✓ **Write consistently.**
  I know people "write when they can," but if you are serious about wanting to finish something, create a writing time every day, and discipline yourself to sit down for say, thirty minutes, or an hour to write. I know some mothers write in ten minute snatches, but for me, I need to have that sitting-in-my-chair time that makes me churn out pages. Some people set page amounts. I write 4000 words a day. But back when I was homeschooling all four kids, it was 1500 a day. I still wrote a 90K novel in sixty days. Divide those sixty days into five days a week, and that would be a total of twelve weeks, or three months! You need to decide: Is writing for you *profession* or *playtime*? The answer will determine how you approach your time.

- ✓ **Do your pre-work.**
  Have your Action/ReAction scene or Action Objectives, your hook, and setting already figured out when you sit down to write. At the end of my previous session, I will have jotted down the Action Objectives of the next scene, defining the element of the Action and ReAction, and who the players might be, and the POV character. I might also have the setting picked out. Since then, I've mulled over a hook in my mind, and perhaps some dialogue. Then, when I sit down, I usually start with a few descriptive words that will define my scene, I review my notes, and then I start writing. Don't surf the net, or answer e-mail, or you won't maximize your time. Be deliberate about this time. Don't even answer the phone!

- ✓ **Schedule "craft" days.**
  Give yourself permission to keep learning.Taking a walk to talk out your character's motivations, or reading "how to write" books are also a good use of time and are essential to grow as a writer. Schedule in "craft" days where all you do is read to learn. This is as important to your writing time as putting the words on the screen.

✓ **Find your balance.**
In the end, we have to remember that God has given us all gifts: home, family, our health, friendship, and the gift to be able to write stories. Be a good steward of all of these. Is your writing becoming an obsession? Are you turning into a workaholic? Is your schedule unbalance—and I don't mean an occasional several days where the house is a dump but a perpetual hey-I-don't-cook-anymore crisis. If you answered "yes" to any (or all) of these questions, then maybe you need to back up and look at how you can reorder your life and make room for each gift that God has given you.

Career Planning!

I'm thrilled that you want to be an author. I love being an author. I love crafting stories, I love seeing my books in Barnes and Noble, and most of all I love getting mail and hearing how my stories have affected readers. I feel like I'm a part of God's big picture in a global way. Cool! But there are some realities that you need to be aware of as you go forward.

Reality Check #1:
Most authors write *four* books before they get one published. Not everyone is John Grisham. Or Stephen King. Or even J.K. Rowling, who, by the way, wrote and rewrote and rewrote Harry Potter before it ever found a publisher. (It was rejected numerous times!) My best advice? After you finish a book and send it into an editor or agent, start another book. You will have learned so much in the writing of the previous book, and you'll want to apply it. Even if you get a rejection, diving into the new book will help keep the dream alive, and maybe even give you insights on how to fix the previous book. Also, when you *do* get published, you'll have an "arsenal" of books ready for your publisher to take a look at, and possibly add to your bookshelf!

By the way, I wrote four books before my first one was published.

Reality Check #2:
Everyone gets rejected, even published authors. And the rejection might not have anything to do with your voice.It might be about timing in the market, or perhaps someone else with a similar book beat you to the publisher. Don't take the rejection personally. Yes, maybe you need to tighten your plot, deepen your characterization, or even ramp up your craft, but the agent or editor doesn't even know you. They only know your story, and their rejection is *not* a rejection of you. Re-evaluate the manuscript with an objective eye, see where you can strengthen it, and dive back in. Or, refer to Reality Check #1 and keep going!

Reality Check #3:
Being published will not make your life easier. Okay, it *is* fun to see your novel on bookstore shelves! But truly, being published only takes your thoughts and puts them out there for the entire world to see. If criticism is tough for you, then you may feel bruised and battered, your dream crushed when (not if!) you read a bad review on Amazon. Being published only makes things harder, in some ways, because your next book has to be better. And likewise, the one after that. The bottom line is: You need to be confident in who you are and what you're about *before* you get published. Because after you're published, you'll have people scrutinizing you in ways you never realized.

Now, how about some Q&A?

Q: There are so many kinds of books out there, and it seems each publisher wants a different thing. Where do I start?

A: Work with publishers who are willing to work with you.

There are many publishers out there who are thrilled to work with new writers—and the list is growing. Heartsong Presents, an imprint of Barbour Publishing has contemporary and historical lines. Love Inspired (an imprint of Steeple Hill) also has historical and contemporary lines, as well as a suspense line. Both these markets are awesome, because they get your books out to a target market who loves to read the genre they order, and not only do you gain experience, but a readership. And it's very fun to walk into a Wal-Mart and see your book sitting on the shelf.

But, you say, I want to write science fiction!

Okay, great. There are two ways most authors' careers grow.

Route 1: Snowball to success. Maybe you have started with a Heartsong book, and grown a readership. Maybe you're also selling to Love Inspired. (Many many authors make a great living selling to just those two lines. They have devoted readers and are reaching people every day.) You could stop there. Or, because that science fiction novel is still in your heart, and because of your numbers and experience you land an agent—and he finds a market that publishes sci-fi. You finally sell the book of your dreams.

Route 2: Go for the big bang. With this route, you work on that manuscript for years and years, submitting that sci-fi, waiting for the market to open, honing your work, winning contests, submitting to agents. You finally get an agent who sees the vision of your story, and you listen to what they say until you get a manuscript they can sell. Then your agent submits it around and finally the sci-fi publisher buys it.

Regardless of the route you've taken, you've spent time honing your work, dreaming the big dream. You've just gone   about it via different routes.

*I write for the same reason
I breathe...because if I
didn't, I would die.*

Isaac Asimov

The Novel in You!

So there you have it! You've discovered and created and are set to publish the novel in you! You should feel proud of all you've done. For one, you can never watch a movie or read a book without asking, "What's his greatest fear?" or, "What's the lie he believes?" And you'll know how to talk intelligently about premise and Black Moments. You'll sound really smart to all your friends! Most of all, when they ask, "Hey, how do you know all that?" you can say, "I learned it *when I wrote my novel*." Cool.

The most important thing is that you've learned the tools to create the *next* novel in you. And the next. And the next!

I hope this book has been helpful. Drop me a line and tell me about your book. And, if you need some personal one-on-one help, check out *My Book Therapy*. We'll help you discover the writer in you!

I want to leave you with *one last secret*:

The My Book Therapy Secret Formula for a Bestselling Book!

> ✓ Explosive two to three chapter opening event (fifty pages)
> ✓ Multifaceted characters with humorous and endearing quirks, favorite foods, music, sayings, hobbies, pet names, and mannerisms.
> ✓ Realistic plot with a make-it-worse for them on all levels: physical, spiritual, emotional (and a happy ending).
> ✓ Storyworld that makes you feel the scene and sense the mood.
> ✓ Backstory in small pieces, culminating to the final scene.
> ✓ Well-researched details that make the story and characters realistic.
> ✓ Thirty pages action and suspense with a homerun ending.
> ✓ Spiritual message that touches the heart.

Congratulations on your novel! And on not quitting until you wrote "The End." Let me know when your book hits the shelves!

Just for fun!

Write the dedication or acknowledgements to your novel:

Pretend you write for *Publisher's Weekly*, and write a review of your book:

Bibliography

(Or the list of books every author should have!)

Getting into Character by Brandilyn Collins
How to Grow a Novel by Sol Stein
Stein on Writing by Sol Stein
Techniques of the Selling Writer by Dwight V. Swain
Plot and Structure by James Scott Bell
Writing the Breakout Novel by Donald Maass
How to Write a (Damn) Good Novel by James Frey

And don't forget to subscribe to the writer's blog at
www.learnhowtowriteanovel.com!

See you on the shelves!

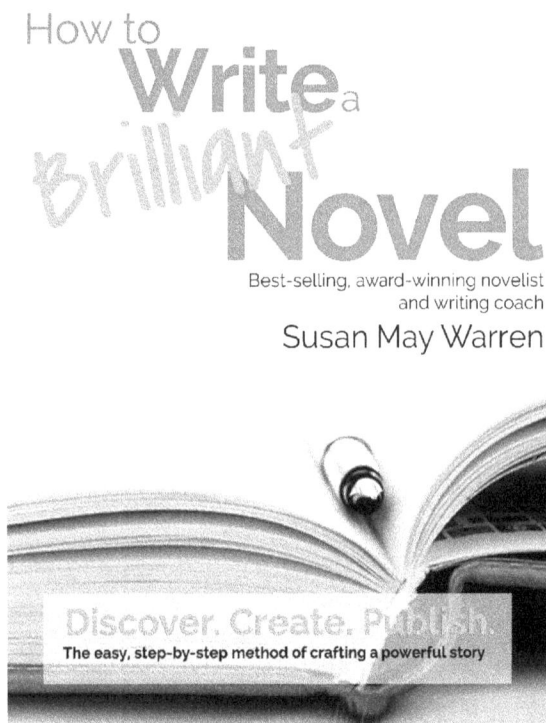

How to Write a Brilliant Novel

The easy, step-by-step method of crafting a powerful story

What does it take to write a brilliant novel? Susan May Warren knows exactly how--and you're about to find out. She's coached hundreds of writers into publication, onto best-seller lists, and onto the awards platforms. (And she lives what she teaches. Susan is the bestselling author of over 50 novels, has won the Rita, the Christy, and the Carol awards multiple times.) Now, for the first time, she's revealing her step-by-step story crafting secrets that will show you how to discover, create, and publish the brilliant novel inside you.

Best-selling, award-winning novelist and writing coach
Susan May Warren

Discover. Create. Publish.
The easy, step-by-step method of crafting a powerful story

Susan's techniques are proven methods that will show you:

- Exactly how bestselling novels are designed

- How to create compelling characters

- How to construct tension-filled scenes. . .that keep readers devouring pagesHow to build sizzling dialogue

- How to develop riveting plots that keep readers guessingAnd once you're finished, how to sell your novel

You CAN Write a Brilliant Novel!

"A quirky, fun, practical guide from a writer who knows what she's doing." -- James Scott Bell, bestselling author of *Write Great Fiction:Plot & Structure*.

Advanced Brilliant Writing

An amazing novel has two elements – deep characterization of a sympathetic hero, and a compelling, wide, breathtaking plot. But how do you create deep characters and wide plots and then apply them to your story? It's time to learn Advanced (Brilliant!) Writing. The follow-up to How to Write a Brilliant Novel, Advanced Brilliant Writing utilizes RITA and Christy award-winning, best-selling novelist Susan May Warren's easy to apply explanations, exercises and intuitive methods to teach you advanced fiction writing techniques that will turn any novel from boring to . . . brilliant.

You'll learn:

- How to plot a profound character change journey

- An easy technique to reveal backstory to your readers

- How to weave emotion into your scene for the most impact

- How to keep tension high through the use of stakes and motivations

- A unique plotting trick to widen your plot

- Techniques on how to make your hero…heroic

- The difference between subplots and layers

- A powerful use for Secondary characters

- How the perfect Villain can help you plot your story

. . . and much more, including the scene that every book MUST have!

"If you're intending to write a best-selling novel, I can think of no better place to start than with Susan May Warren's Deep and Wide. This is a book for those who need to dig into the techniques of writing -- not just hear the happy-talk, big-picture stuff that is so often heard at conferences. If you really want to get into the nuts and bolts of writing strong fiction, then this is for you. Clear, practical advice from an award-winning novelist." *Chip MacGregor, Literary Agent, MacGregor Literary*

Advanced
Brilliant
Writing

Best-selling, award-winning novelist and writing coach
Susan May Warren

Make your plot wider and your characters deeper.

My Brilliant Book Buddy

Best-selling, award-winning novelist
and writing coach
Susan May Warren

You've got a friend in me

The easy, step-by-step manuscript companion

My Brilliant Book Buddy

The writing journey can be long and lonely. It's easy to get lost in the weeds of your story, not sure where you are headed . . . or why. Wouldn't it be nice to have a guide along the way? Someone to point you in the right direction, and keep you motivated.

A manuscript companion to the foundational writer's workbook How to Write a Brilliant Novel, and advanced writer's guide, Advanced Brilliant Writing, My Brilliant Book Buddy puts feet to all the steps needed to create a powerful book, guiding you through character creation, plotting the inner and outer journey, creating essential scenes, and word-painting. With step-by-step instruction, it helps you craft the perfect black moment, and pushes you on all the way to the climatic ending.

"The Book Buddy is my new best friend! It takes all of the helpful tools, charts and tips from Inside Out and Deep and Wide and puts them in one place. It's like having Susan May Warren in the room helping you craft your story! I can't recommend it highly enough! *Melissa Tagg, multi-published romance author*

How to
Write a
Brilliant
Romance

Best-selling, award-winning novelist
and writing coach
Susan May Warren

Why do fools fall in love?
The easy, step-by-step method of crafting a powerful romance

How to Write a Brilliant Romance

The easy, step-by-step method of crafting a powerful romance

What does it take to write a brilliant romance? Susan May Warren knows exactly how--and you're about to find out.

Now, for the first time, she's revealing her step-by-step romance writing secrets that will show you how to craft an award-winning romance.

Secrets like:

- How do I structure my romance?

- How do I create likeable heroes and heroines?

- How should my hero and heroine meet?

- How do I make two characters fall in love?

- How do I write a sizzling kiss?

- How do I create believable conflict?

- How do I keep the tension high in the middle of my story?

- How do I put romance on every page?

- What is the breakup and why do I need it?

- Most importantly, how do I create an unique romance that touches the heart of my reader?

Find the answers to all these questions as well as a few secrets to creating award-winning romances.

With ten ingredients and step by step instructions you'll learn how to plot and write a powerful, layered romance designed to win readers. Susan May Warren has coached hundreds of writers into publication, onto best-seller lists, and onto the awards platforms. (And she lives what she teaches. Susan is the bestselling author of over 50 novels, has won the Rita, the Christy, and the Carol awards multiple times.)

Did you like this book? Thank you for reading!

I love to help authors with their craft, encouraging them and
equipping them with tools to get published and stay published. I do hope you enjoyed our "conversations" and that they
helped you as you grew your story.

If you're interested in more resources on writing craft, or even growing your career as a novelist, check out our website:
www.mybooktherapy.com. Sign up to receive the daily dose of writing craft, and check out our programs and/or events. We have something for everyone!

If this book clicked with you, I'd be ever so grateful if you'd
share that with me (susan@mybooktherapy.com) and others by way of a review on Amazon.com.

Go – write something brilliant!